Living the *Intuitive* Life
Cultivating Extraordinary Awareness

Living the *Intuitive* Life
Cultivating Extraordinary Awareness

Tonya Madia, RYT, RMT, LMBT

Foreword by William Douglas Horden

Visionary Living, Inc.
New Milford, Connecticut

Living the Intuitive Life:
Cultivating Extraordinary Awareness

By Tonya Madia, RYT, RMT, LMBT

Copyright Tonya Madia, 2017

Published by Visionary Living, Inc.
New Milford, Connecticut
www.visionaryliving.com

All rights reserved.
No part of this book may be reproduced in any form or used without permission.

Front cover design by Chuck Regan
Back cover and interior design by Leslie McAllister

ISBN: 978-1-942157-19-9 (pbk)
ISBN: 978-1-942157-20-5 (epub)

Published by Visionary Living, Inc.
New Milford, Connecticut
www.visionaryliving.com

To my wonderful husband Joey for always believing in me and helping me find my way back to my Magical Child.

Acknowledgments

Like anything worth doing in life, the pursuit of the Intuitive Life is mostly about relationships, so any book that did not take time to thank the people who have contributed most to my learning to love and accept myself would be incredibly lacking.

My grandmother, Clara Donath. Thank you for always setting an example of what it means to fearlessly be yourself, and also for introducing me to the many ways in which one can explore and cultivate their natural intuitive ability.

My aunt, Denise Wall. Thank you for your unwavering support and love. It is because of you that I have managed to find my way through many difficult times.

My children, Daniel, Jeremy, and Jolie; you have taught me more about life and love than you will ever know.

My aunt, Annette Becker. There are no words to express what your unconditional love and guidance have contributed to my life. It is because of you that I found my way off the sissy path and on to the path to my Authentic Self.

My friend, Michelle Bowser, for never questioning a single experience that I've shared and for always being up for any conversation, no matter how far down the rabbit hole it leads.

My mentors, William and Leonor Horden. Your guidance and support have contributed more to my development than I could ever express.

My friends Rosemary Ellen Guiley—thank you for helping me believe that I could write this book and investing the time and energy into ensuring its success; Vicki Angotti—thank you for encouraging me to pursue my Reiki training; Lory Osborn and Marti Shamberger—you were the first friends I met on my path to Authenticity. Your unfailing support and encouragement have meant more to me than you will ever know; LeLa Becker—for giving me the courage to become a Yoga teacher; Joanne Vandenhengel— your contributions to my life are too many to mention; Phyllis and John Griggs—your support and spiritual guidance have been invaluable to my ability to find my way to the non-sissy path; Elizabeth Halliday Reynolds—for creating a place for light-workers to find their path and for your invaluable support and friendship; and John and Tim Frick and Steve Ward—for all you have taught me over the years.

Table of Contents

Dedication   v
Acknowledgments   vii
Foreword Introduction   xi

1. What is That Little Voice and Where is It Coming From?   1
2. Intuition and the Entangled Mind   11
3. Human Energy Systems and Energy as Information   25
4. The Intuitive Life and the Clairs   43
5. Strange Visitations from "Ghostesses" and Other Spirits   65
6. Developing Intuition in the Field   81
7. Creating a Strong Energy Body   93
8. Dreamwork and the Language of Symbols   113
9. Signs, Synchronicities and Working with Your Guides   131
10. Implementing Tools for Guidance and Protection   149
11. Putting It All Together and Living the Intuitive Life   169

About the Author   179
Bibliography   181

Foreword

To meet and spend time with Tonya Madia—as has been my pleasure—is to encounter a most enjoyable paradox. On the one hand, she is a gentle, soft-spoken and open-hearted person who connects readily with others on an emotional soul level and, on the other, a voracious researcher with a keen mind quick to distil complex concepts into intelligible everyday language. One trait, however, shines through both these facets of Tonya's personality: a spiritual sincerity as eager to listen and learn as to share and teach.

All these qualities are in abundant display in the book you hold in your hands. Here you will find Tonya's heart and soul laid bare in personal stories and carefully arrived at lessons from her experiences. Here, too, you will find a veritable reference book of resources to guide you toward the practices that most resonate with your path in the intuitive life. And, perhaps most valuable, here you will find a treasure trove of practical exercises to enhance the cultivation of your intuition.

I encourage you to meet and spend time with Tonya Madia as she accompanies you through this landscape, both wondrously ancient and modern, of the archetypal world of the collective imagination and its individual embodiment, *The Intuitive Life*.

—William Douglas Horden
Ithaca, Spring 2017

Introduction

The world is but a canvas to the imagination. **Henry David Thoreau**

Imagination will often carry us to worlds that never were. But without it we go nowhere. **Carl Sagan**

The Intuitive Life is the magical life. It is a life of pure wonder and amazement. It is a life lived outside of fear, where everything you take in is amazingly and wonderfully magical.

Before we begin, let's take a moment and send ourselves back to our childhoods, to the carefree days of lying in the grass and gazing up at the clouds in search of elephants, dragons and other magical creatures. Take yourself back to the days when every tree branch called out to be explored, each day held new adventures and every moment shared a common denominator: pure potential. Allow yourself to spend some time in this place, where every ring of the telephone held the possibility for a call to adventure and each moment revealed its potential for magic. Remember yourself as a child, when you saw beauty in all things, understood the power of imagination and believed that anything was possible. That child was the embodiment of the Magical Child archetype and that child still resides within you.

Remember those days spent dwelling in amazement and awe, so filled with wonder that it was, well… wonder-FUL. Inhale deeply and as you breathe in, remember this feeling, and hold it in your mind and heart, because this is what it feels like to live the Intuitive Life.

When you were a child you did this naturally, effortlessly; you didn't need to read a book about how to do it because you were born *knowing* it. It was intuitive!

Perhaps you never forgot this feeling and continue to dwell completely in it every moment of every day. If so, send this book to someone in your life who needs its exercises, explorations, and encouragement, and go have fun, because you don't need it. But, if you're like most people, and you don't find yourself swimming in magic and wonder, keep reading—this book was truly written for you. It's going to be a lot of fun but you will need to be brave, because I have to tell you from the outset that this journey is not for sissies. I know because I've been on this journey my entire life, much of which I spent taking the sissy route. Not only was it not wonder-FUL, it wasn't even interesting. I'm not sure exactly when I stepped foot on the sissy path, but somewhere along the way, I allowed my desire to "fit in" and my fear of being different to pull me away from the elephants, dragons, tree-tops and calls to adventure to settle for the safety of conformity.

At that moment, I stepped out of the realm of childhood wonder and magic and into the realm of the mundane. I stopped being guided by what I sensed and felt in every moment and started listening to the advice of those who had long since stepped off the intuitive path to settle for ordinary lives resembling those of everyone else around them. Fortunately for me, I encountered mentors along the way who would carefully guide me back toward adventure and the path to Extraordinary Awareness and Authenticity. It's an amazing adventure in which each day holds new and endless possibilities. It is fascinating and exhilarating and it looks very little like the life you were led to believe you should live. It will require that you be courageous and embrace your vulnerability, but if you're willing to let go of the smallness of conformity I promise the rewards are no less than extraordinary.

The Intuitive Life is the playful life. My favorite moments are those in which I allow my inner child to explore and create. I found myself thinking about this recently while I was enjoying a swim at my local gym. It was a quiet, rainy afternoon and I had the whole pool to myself. As I was doing laps, I began to get bored and noticed my thoughts arising and taking me out of the moment, diminishing my enjoyment of the swim. Remembering times spent playing in the pool when I was a child, I decided that I was going to allow my imagination to take over and see what creative inspirations and archetypal messages might arise for me.

What arose was an exciting adventure in which I was a mermaid in search of a monkey who had been tragically thrown into the depths of the ocean. I was on a mission to find and rescue the monkey, and as I swam through tangles of seaweed, hidden mazes and obstacles, I found myself wondering why it is that we abandon our imaginations and sense of play in exchange for boring and mundane existences. Happy that I had long since reclaimed my ability to play, I dove under again, this time locating the monkey next to a mound of golden treasure. (You might be asking yourself why the monkey didn't drown, but don't trouble yourself about that; the wonderful thing about imagination is that ANYTHING is possible!)

As I enjoyed my creative rescue mission in the pool, the gym's maintenance man stepped out of the locker room and I suppose he couldn't help but notice that instead of swimming laps like a normal adult, I appeared to be engaged in some kind of play (diving and splashing about as I was). He stood there staring at me, his head tilted to one side, his gaze frozen in bewilderment. I wanted to call out to him, "I'm rescuing a monkey! Come and join me! Help me find the monkey!"

I didn't. I just smiled at him and continued with my rescue as he scratched his head and walked away. As I returned to my adventure, it occurred to me that being open in the moment, allowing our imaginations to work their magic, is a large part of living the Intuitive Life. Although imagination and intuition are separate functions, they are closely related and they both communicate in the same language, the language of symbols. When we allow ourselves the opportunity to engage in imaginative play or creativity we are becoming fluent in the language of symbols.

Another skill that imagination allows us to develop is that of trust. When we engage in the realm of imagination, we tend to just go with what arises. My adventure in the pool is a good example of this.

"Rescue a monkey in the depths of the ocean?"

"Sure!"

No need to worry about silly details like oxygen, no need to question why a mermaid, or why a monkey. It's just play! (Some readers may recognize the tale of Hanuman the Monkey and Suvannamaccha the Mermaid from the *Ramayana*.) If you think back to your cloud-gazing days, you might recall that as you lay in the grass next to your friends or siblings you didn't worry about what they would think if your cloud was decidedly a turtle. It just was a turtle and you weren't worried about what anyone thought about it. You didn't have to defend it. This is what it takes to cultivate your intuition. No second-guessing. No worrying. Just trusting your instincts and learning to recognize them when they arise.

Last, reacquainting yourself with imaginative play serves to shift you into a state of mind that provides fertile ground for intuition, a state of openness and wonder. If this book does nothing else I hope that it delivers to you the message that it is okay to play, to have fun, and to delve into the depths of your creative waters and splash around in search of your monkey and the hidden treasures awaiting you. Let go of any concerns that you may have about what other grown-ups might think about your behavior, and allow yourself to be free the way that you were when you were a child.

Just outside the realm that you have become accustomed to dwelling in is another realm, a realm of amazing possibilities inhabited by symbols, archetypes, and mystical beings. A realm in which information about anything you wish to know is readily available to you, and you are about to learn how to access it.

Living the Intuitive Life means understanding your relationship with the amazing world around you. You are a living, breathing symbol in constant interaction with the other living symbols in and around you.

Are you ready to let go and play?

1

WHAT IS THAT LITTLE VOICE AND WHERE IS IT COMING FROM?

Everyone who wills can hear the inner voice. It is within everyone.
Mahatma Gandhi

Your mind knows only some things. Your inner voice, your instinct, knows everything. If you listen to what you know instinctively, it will always lead you down the right path. **Henry Winkler**

Within us all there is a little voice of wisdom that, if we trust and follow it, will lead us in the right direction. It is the job or investment opportunity that you somehow knew you had to pass up, it is the trip you cancelled at the last minute because something about it didn't "feel quite right," it is the person you met once and immediately felt a strong connection to, or the nagging feeling that insists that you contact an old friend you haven't spoken to in years.

At one time or another, we have all experienced the quiet guidance of our own intuition in the form of that "inner voice," guidance that protected us from danger or prevented us from making disastrous mistakes. There are countless stories of people (including two of my uncles) who were supposed to show up for work or a meeting at the Twin Towers on September 11, 2001 and cancelled their meetings or called in sick because of a feeling of uneasiness they experienced. I've also heard stories of people who, compelled by a gut feeling and subtle inner voice, took an alternate route to avoid a bridge on the day it collapsed.

There are several accounts of individuals who were set to board RMS *Titanic* but because of premonitions or dreams about people drowning, decided to cancel their reservations. Major Archibald Willingham Butt had a premonition that he would not return home from his journey across the Atlantic, yet he did not cancel his reservation aboard the ill-fated ship. He instead contacted his lawyer to arrange his last will and testament prior to the ship's maiden voyage. The Major was among the 1500 souls lost to the sea in 1912 on that cold April morning.

I not only notice stories like this as I continue to cultivate my own Intuitive Life; I collect them. They remind me to trust and to believe that there are larger forces at work that I am able to tap into and receive guidance from. There are lots of stories in this book to get you started on your own collection; I encourage you to write down your own, and begin to collect others' as well.

The amazing inner voice that we all possess is a valuable tool, but it doesn't only steer us away from danger and discomfort; when we are willing to pay attention, it often steers us toward opportunities, windfalls and love. One of my most cherished encounters with my inner voice occurred not long before one the wise mentors who would gently guide me back to the Intuitive Life would enter my life.

In 1997, I was a single mother, living in Arizona, when, out of the blue, having never performed in my life, an intensely burning desire to be in a play suddenly overcame me. I couldn't explain it and yet, at the same time, I couldn't ignore it. I suppose you would have had to know me back then to fully understand exactly how out of character this was for me, but suffice it to say, at the time, I probably would have preferred to have had my lungs extracted with a spoon than to stand, vulnerable, on a stage in front of a large group of people. Not just people; *strangers*.

Yet, a little voice inside continued to press me to search the local paper for theatrical opportunities. *Immediately and right away*, the voice insisted, and to my amazement, I opened the paper to discover that an audition for the play *Lost in Yonkers* was to be held the following week by a local community theater. As terrified as I was at the prospect of standing on a stage, the compulsion to audition was so strong that I simply had to follow through with it, mingled though it was with notions of how the spoon scenario might be a bit less frightening and feel slightly less painful.

A week later, I nervously made my way into a little Scottsdale theater and printed my name on the sign-in sheet that had been handed to me by the silver-haired lady behind the counter. In retrospect, it was incredible that I managed to make it through the audition, considering that I was so riddled with self-doubt that it seemed to be pulsating through my veins. All the while my doubt reminded me that almost anything in the world would feel more comfortable than standing alone on stage, in a room filled with "real actors"—people who had done this sort of thing before, and in front of a scrutinizing stranger with a clipboard.

As frightening as it was, in the end, the inner voice that had insisted I undertake this endeavor prevailed. I read from the script that I had been presented with, while all the while being painfully aware of the glaring pairs of eyeballs blinking in my direction.

When I was finished I thanked the director and, red-faced and flustered, abruptly made my way out of the building. As I drove home, the little voice inside assured me I had done the right thing and I let out a sigh, feeling confident that the point of the whole thing was just that I overcome my fear of being on stage. Obviously, one of the experienced actresses would land the part, I thought, but I was left with the satisfaction of following through with something that, previously, I was certain, I would never be able to do. I was stunned beyond belief when, upon arriving home, I learned that I had been cast in the lead role of the production.

Two months later, just after the show closed, I met my future husband in the lobby of that little theater. Joey had just flown in from New Jersey after a persistent voice within *him* had insisted that a multi-week trip out west to see old theater friends would be just the thing to help mend his recently broken heart. According to his mother and other family members, this was just as out of character for him as my auditioning for the play.

As we were being introduced, I couldn't ignore the feeling that I remembered Joey from somewhere, not recognized so much, but *remembered*. As we shook hands, that little voice inside me whispered, *It's you, there you are!* As Joey and I got to know each other over the next few months, it became clear that in addition to common interests, we shared amazingly similar childhood experiences, and even more, we shared a connection on a fundamental level within us… a connection on a soul level. I believe that this was the recognition reflected to me in Joey's eyes on the day we met.

In a perfect synchronicity for a book like this, we are doing the final edit of this chapter on May 8—exactly 20 years to the day that we had our first date—all because I listened to the little voice that told me to audition for a play.

We were married seven months later, against the urging and advice from friends and family who thought that we should wait. They were convinced that we had lost our marbles, or at the very least were being irrational and impulsive. In retrospect, I suppose we were (being impulsive that is, the lost marble part might still be up for debate, but in all fairness who hasn't misplaced an occasional marble here or there?). However, our willingness to listen to that inner voice and follow where it led has rewarded us with a beautiful daughter, my two sons with a caring, devoted father, and 20 years of friendship and romance.

As amazing as our story is, it is actually not at all uncommon. One of our favorite ways of getting to know new couples is by asking them how they met, and we are rarely disappointed. Time and time again we've heard the tale of mysterious inner voices leading two lonely hearts toward each other under unusual and often charming circumstances. It is so common in fact that it is part of the formula used by screenwriters when creating romantic comedies, and is affectionately referred to as the "meet cute." In order for the meet cute to work its magic, however, we must first trust and follow that inner voice, our intuition.

Intuition is something we are all born with; it is a natural part of the human condition. All animals possess intuition, and human beings are no different. Before the advent of modern technology, early humans not only had faith in their inner voice, they depended on it to survive. They understood that when trusted, their inner voice would lead them to water, shelter, food, and to healing plants; they relied on it to alert them of danger and lead them to their next meal.

As our dependence on science and technology grew, and our connection with nature dwindled, we began to rely less on that inner voice, often dismissing it as fancy or imagination. Reliance on modern technology isn't the only reason for this loss. From the time we are small children, we are conditioned to put our faith only in what can be seen, heard, and felt. Little whispering voices upon meeting someone are not to be trusted, and gut feelings, as accurate as they often are, are not to be shared or discussed, lest we be considered to be wanting in the ole' marble department. As a result, as we grow up, we begin to ignore our inner voice and dismiss our own gut feelings. When we lose our connection to nature, we not only lose our connection to our inner voice, but our inner child as well. The Magical Child who sees beauty everywhere, understands the sacredness inherent in nature, and believes that anything is possible. I believe that the Magical Child and the inner voice are closely connected and for this reason the Intuitive Life requires that we find ways to reconnect with and spend time in nature.

I think that grandmothers understand this. I am fairly certain that I have never met a grandmother who has not learned to reconnect with, and listen to, her inner voice.

Grandmas just seem to *know*; you can't fool them. Grandma can take one look at you and that little inner voice of hers will tell her if you are hungry, sad, upset, or guilty. Don't try to fool her; she knows what you need, and, I am sorry to say, what you have been up to.

I was very fortunate to have a grandmother who had not only mastered her intuitive abilities, but had also spent most of her adult life studying and cultivating them. My grandmother Clara was fearless. She marched to the beat of her own drum and she never worried what others thought of her. To say that Clara was colorful and unique would be an understatement. She boldly dared to be herself every moment of every day and even those who had trouble understanding her had to admit she had a flare all her own. For her, the sissy path was never an option. Clara was completely comfortable living the Intuitive Life. She understood her own intuitive abilities and was very familiar with how to tap into those abilities. She frequently sought guidance from tools such as meditation, guided visualization, and automatic writing, and I spent much of my young life watching in fascination as she shared her experiences with me. I wasn't quite as brave as my grandmother, so it wouldn't be until much later that I would learn to trust and cultivate my own intuitive abilities. Once I began marching to the rhythm of my own drum I found the teachings she had shared with me over the years to be invaluable.

I suspect that grandmas begin to reconnect with their intuition when they become mothers. Any mother will tell you that she has strong instincts about her children. That type of knowing begins from the time our children arrive and their tiny swaddled bodies are placed into our arms. As they grow, so does our sixth sense about them, so that by the time our children receive their own precious, swaddled parcels, we have practically transformed ourselves into intuitive masters.

Much like mothers, fathers develop their own intuitive abilities about their children. My husband is one of the most intuitive persons I know, and to my recollection he has never been mistaken about a first impression, although, regrettably, he hasn't always paid attention to them. When it comes to our three children, in situations that I know there is something going on with one of them, he usually has a pretty strong sense about what that *something* is. I think the main difference between men and women when it comes to intuition is our approach. Joey will wait patiently for the kids to come to him for advice or guidance, while I will just blurt out my concerns in the form of questions like "What's wrong?" or "Is everything ok?" Though I often know the answer, my prodding rarely produces the information that I am seeking.

Grandfathers, I believe, continue with this subtler approach. Grandpas know when it's time to go for a walk, go fishing, share a soda together, or just sit and watch a sunset. It is in those quiet moments that grandpas can uncover the wonderful mysteries about us that we were never even aware existed, and at the same time teach us valuable life lessons under the guise of how to bait a fishing line.

If you're not a parent, don't worry. Aunts, uncles, brothers, sisters, sons, and daughters all seem to possess the same intuitive abilities whenever close bonds exist. As wonderful as these familial instincts are, they often don't translate to other areas of our lives. We tend to ignore that voice within, or become so distracted by outside stimuli that we simply don't hear it, and by doing so, might be missing out on incredible opportunities and fortuitous "meet cutes." The exciting news is that because these abilities are something that we are all born with, anyone can learn to cultivate and master their natural intuitive abilities. In the same way that anyone can be taught to play an instrument or learn a foreign language we can all be taught how to recognize and develop intuitive abilities.

With so much anecdotal evidence surrounding the intuitive inner voice, there is a widespread acceptance within our society about its existence. If asked, most people would agree that, at one time or another, when they have chosen to trust rather than dismiss it, they have experienced the benefit of listening to their own inner voice.

However, explaining the source of that inner voice becomes a difficult challenge.

During a 1994 United Nations presentation to members of the Society for Enlightenment and Transformation, author, artist, intuitive, and researcher Ingo Swann asked, "How many of you here today would like to know you have at least 17 senses rather than just five of them? How many think that 17 would be better than just five? How many of you here already know that you have more than five senses?"

Ingo Swann followed his question by revealing discoveries made during his years involved in government research including the discovery of bioelectric sensors not only in the skin, but in the neuropeptide activity that transmits information into the brain and back into the body's extremities, its internal organs, and into its surrounding bioelectromagnetic field. Known as the father of remote viewing, Swann, along with physicist Russell Targ, was fundamental in the development of the Remote viewing protocols established by the Stanford Research Institute and delivered to the US military as a remote viewing training methodology.

Additionally, Swann spoke of what those additional senses are, stating that the soles of our feet and the palms of our hands contain minute magnetic receptors and sensors that "recognize" minute and gross changes in local magnetism. He pointed out that since you haven't built neural pathways linking these sensors to your cognitive faculties, you probably won't be able to sense what the receptors in the soles of your feet are picking up. I believe that it is these pathways that create for us a quality of consciousness that exists outside the realm of our ordinary awareness, and allow us to perceive subtle bits of information that are then conveyed to us through the mechanism of the inner voice.

I will talk more about Ingo Swann and Russell Targ and their fascinating research with Project Stargate in later chapters; however, since a complete exploration of their work is beyond the scope of this book, I encourage readers to read the detailed accounts of their experiences through their works: *Reality Boxes and Other Black Holes in Human Consciousness*, by Ingo Swann, and *Limitless Mind: A Guide to Remote Viewing and Transformation of Consciousness* and *The Reality of ESP: A Physicist's Proof of Psychic Abilities*, by Russell Targ.

Because the analytic mind prefers to be in charge, it always seeks to quiet and overrule the inner voice by labeling, questioning, judging, and very often dismissing information received through the sensing systems identified by Ingo Swann. Learning to tune into these systems so that we can receive input from the inner voice not only enhances our day-to-day experiences but enriches our personal relationships as well.

Cultivating an Intuitive Life is a process that requires the purposeful shift of our awareness from the ordinary and mundane to the extraordinary and unexpected. It is a return to the feeling associated with the wonder and magic of childhood, and is only possible when we allow ourselves to let go of our concerns for what others might think and allow ourselves to reconnect with our hearts. Extraordinary Awareness is cultivated through creative play and the use of the imagination and is achieved through a process of breathing, listening, feeling, understanding, and trusting… simultaneously. Once mastered, Extraordinary Awareness becomes our natural state and we begin to dwell in the magical state of wonder that was so readily available to us as children. Once this shift has occurred, every day becomes an adventure and every moment holds the potential of infinite possibilities. Dwelling in Extraordinary Awareness is only the beginning; in this state, we can tune into the sensing systems referred to by Ingo Swann. We become receivers for the energetic information that surrounds us, and we can begin to learn how to decode and apply the symbolic messages that are now readily available to us.

When it was first suggested that I write a book about learning to trust and apply intuition, I wondered what, with so many excellent books already available, I might possibly add to the topic. My desire is to offer my own extraordinary experiences and unique perspective, with the hope that I might help the reader readily recognize, trust, cultivate, and apply their own unique intuitive abilities to their daily lives. It is also my hope to offer a slightly different perspective about the nature of reality. I hope that you will allow yourself (if only for the time it takes to read this book) to accept that there are things in this world that cannot be explained and that science is only now beginning to recognize. More than anything I hope to remind you that life does not have to be boring and mundane, it is okay to use your imagination and play, and it is a requirement of all non-sissies everywhere to bravely and creatively be themselves, every moment of every day.

The exercises provided in this book are designed to help you learn the process of shifting in to Extraordinary Awareness, which in turn allows your intuition to tell your thinking mind where to look next. Perhaps it's in your local paper for an audition announcement…

It is my hope that this book might help you to develop the confidence to forego your fears regarding how many marbles you may, or may not be, in possession of, at least when it comes to listening to your inner voice. When it comes to developing any relationship, even those with your own inner voice, trust is absolutely essential, and it is difficult, if not all together impossible, to listen to that subtle, guiding voice if one is preoccupied with counting marbles.

2

Intuition and the Entangled Mind

One really should start thinking in terms of biomind receptors, rather than in terms of ESP. **Ingo Swann**

John Bell gave us a mathematical proof that our space-time reality is nonlocal—whether we like it or not. **Russell Targ**

We arrive on this planet with our intuitive faculties in full working order and with our bioreceptors ready to receive signals from our surrounding environment. Anyone who has ever tried to calm a crying infant while feeling stressed or impatient has experienced firsthand how well these receptors work for babies. No matter how soothing the words, melodic the song or cooing the voice, it will have little calming affect for an infant who is receiving conflicting energetic signals from a frazzled caregiver.

As they grow into toddlers, their empathic ability to perceive important information about their caregivers remains. When my children were very small I was always delighted when, after a long or trying day, they would be especially affectionate, climbing into my lap and offering more hugs, kisses, and snuggles than usual. In doing so, my children were not only offering me much needed emotional support, but physiological support as well. Studies reveal that human touch increases the release of oxytocin, a neuropeptide often referred to as the "love hormone." Oxytocin promotes feelings of devotion and bonding and is known to lower both blood pressure and cortisol (a hormone released in response to stress).

One of my favorite stories to tell about my son Jeremy has to do with the first time he met my husband Joey. Although he didn't let it show, Joey was anxious at the prospect of meeting my children. Jeremy, who was two at the time, took one look at Joey and asked, "Can I have a hug?" That hug went a long way toward easing Joey's anxieties, and was the initial spark of a bond that would develop between a father and his soon-to-be son. Although Jeremy may not have fully understood the reason he felt so compelled to request a hug from a complete stranger, the little voice within him made it clear that a hug was needed.

What exactly are these intuitive abilities that we are born with? The ability to sense or know something without need for conscious reasoning is commonly referred to as intuition, psychic experience, extra sensory perception (ESP), or "psi." In the scientific field, these abilities are often referred to as *anomalous cognition*. For centuries, Eastern philosophies have referred to these abilities as *Siddhis*, or exceptional abilities, which are refined through strict dedication to practices such as yoga, meditation and purification. Masters of these practices are called *Sadhus*.

Studies done over the past several decades have shown that quite a large number of people report having had "psychic experiences" involving such psi phenomena as precognition, telepathy, and clairvoyance. Although many relegate these abilities to the realms of mysticism, superstition, and the supernatural, they are, in fact, abilities that we all possess, and strengthening and cultivating these abilities can be done through training, practice, exercising imagination, and the cultivating of Extraordinary Awareness.

Take a moment to give some thought to what the word "intuition" means to you. Call to mind some experiences you have had in which you experienced intuition and as you do so, spend some time journaling about what you are hoping to gain from reading this book. Keeping a journal about your day-to-day experiences with intuition is a wonderful way to learn more about how this faculty works for you, and now is the perfect time to start one specifically for the work you will do through the exercises from this book and the work you will continue to do beyond it. This will be your Extraordinary Awareness journal.

I have yet to meet anyone in the course of my life who has never had experiences in which they seemed to intuit, dream, or "know" something without any explanation as to why. A large percentage of such incidents occur in dreams, while synchronicities, or "meaningful coincidences," are also very common. Additionally, many people report experiencing such (seemingly) unexplained phenomena as having encounters with deceased loved ones or experiencing haunting activity. The problem is not that these experiences are rare—they aren't—but that people are conditioned from a young age not to talk about them and, as the conditioning continues, to dismiss them out of hand or explain them away as the result of an "overactive imagination."

Although intuiting something (thinking of your friend at the exact moment that she calls you, for example, as often happens with my friend Michelle) and seeing a ghost are slightly different faculties, they are both the result of the bioelectric sensors identified by Ingo Swann. I like to think of them as two fingers of the same hand. We all experience subtle energies in our surrounding environments in a variety of different ways and those ways are as unique and varied as the individual experiencing them. You may not be reading this book because you have a desire to learn to "intuit" or see ghosts or spirits; in fact, you may have never even thought about such a possibility. Cultivating your Extraordinary Awareness doesn't necessarily have to include learning to tune into those frequencies. On the other hand, some of us are born with a stronger natural capacity for doing so that causes this to happen whether we like the idea or not. I liken it to natural music or athletic ability. Some of us are naturally born with a tendency toward being musicians or athletes. I, sadly enough, was not born with either an inherently strong musical or athletic ability; instead, the universe saw fit to infuse me with natural clairvoyant abilities—something I was not always terribly happy about.

Regardless of whether you would like to cultivate your intuitive abilities to simply enhance your life through the quiet guidance of your helpful inner voice, or whether you are hoping to tap into and understand the workings of such faculties as clairvoyance, the process is the same and it is up to you where you would like this book to take you.

Working with the exercises in the chapters that follow will help you know what is right for you.

Although science has yet to provide a full explanation for the way in which the human body perceives such subtle information as the emotional experience of those around us, knowing when our friend will call, or seeing apparitions, I believe that the field of quantum physics comes very close, and will eventually provide us with an explanation for this phenomenon.

In the field of quantum physics, it is understood that there is a fundamental interconnectedness, or *entanglement*, of subatomic particles. In a 1947 letter to German physicist Max Born, Albert Einstein referred to this quantum-interconnectedness as "spooky action at a distance," describing the phenomenon of two entangled particles influencing each other across great distances.

In 1964 CERN physicist John Stewart Bell provided mathematical proof of this phenomenon, which he referred to as "nonlocality." According to quantum mechanics, elementary particles, rather than existing in a single location, are actually spread out, existing in multiple locations at once. In addition, these particles inexplicably pop in and out of existence, and become entangled with one another even when they are light-years apart.

Recognizing our entanglement on a subatomic level brings us one step closer to understanding the way in which our bioelectrical bodies receive and process information about our environment and the people around us. One of the biggest challenges, however, in discovering the exact nature in which these processes work is that is it impossible to duplicate spontaneous occurrences of intuition within the cold, controlled setting of a laboratory. Physicist Russell Targ did feel, however, that his decades of Remote viewing research came close to providing more answers.

"Remote viewing" is a term coined by Ingo Swann. Stanford Research Institute (SRI) International defined it in the *Coordinate Remote Viewing Training Manual (CRV Manual)* as "the acquisition and description, by mental means, of information blocked from ordinary perception by distance, shielding, or time."

In a remote viewing session, the "viewer" attempts to acquire and describe information about a designated location or target. The viewer has no knowledge or information about the site or target that must be described. When a friend introduced me to the process of remote viewing several years ago I could hardly contain my excitement. Finally, I thought, a process that has been studied and developed that brings light into the way that sensing abilities work. I wanted to learn more and began reading all the books and articles I could find and watching any recorded lecture I could get my hands on.

In 1972 Dr. Hal Puthoff, a physicist at SRI, conducted an experiment with psychic Ingo Swann that attracted attention and funding from the Central Intelligence Agency (CIA). Russell Targ subsequently joined the team and the psi research that Swann would later term "remote viewing" began. In their experiments, coordinates to unknown locations were provided to viewers who could describe top-secret locations with stunning accuracy.

Project Stargate was the codename for these experiments, which were conducted by the US government for over 20 years. The project was established at Fort Meade, Maryland, by the Defense Intelligence Agency

(DIA) and SRI International after US intelligence sources discovered that the Soviet Union was engaging in psychical research. Not to be outdone by the Russians, the CIA initiated funding for a new program known as SCANATE ("scan by coordinate") and the Remote viewing research began in 1972 at SRI.

Because of his contributions to the project, Ingo Swann became known as the "father of remote viewing." Respected for his extraordinary accuracy within laboratory settings, Swann eventually worked with more than 38 researchers in the fields of parapsychology and cognitive perception. Remote viewer Paul H. Smith, PhD, wrote of Ingo Swann:

"Over the course of his career, Swann not only introduced revolutionary new ways of thinking about consciousness research, but created what is today probably the most successful and widely-used method of teaching the practical use of consciousness-based skills. In accomplishing those purposes, he himself performed uncountable thousands of remote viewing sessions in support of research, training, and operational goals."

Ingo Swann advocated a systematic and deliberate approach to the development of psi ability, and preferred the term Distant Mental Interactions with Living Systems (DMILS) to ESP. Swann described the human sensory apparatus as a "transducer array" to convert information from one form to another, and referred to the human "software" program as a "mental information processing grid."

Remote viewing is based on the premise that expanding the parameters of perception is a skill that can be taught. The information obtained through remote viewing is thought to be carried to the viewer via a "signal line," and is detected by the viewer's subconscious. The remote viewing protocols established by Ingo Swann are designed to facilitate the transfer of information from the viewer's subconscious to waking consciousness, where it can be interpreted. This process is implemented through a protocol, which leads to increasingly deeper states of consciousness, allowing the viewer to establish a greater connection with the signal line.

The *CRV Manual* describes the signal line as "the hypothesized train of signals emanating from the Matrix and perceived by the remote viewer, which transports the information obtained through the Remote viewing process." The manual goes on to describe the Matrix as "a huge, non-material, highly structured, mentally accessible 'framework' of information containing all data, and pertaining to everything in both the physical and non-physical universe."

The signal line is a carrier wave, analogous to radio waves which radiate in many different frequencies and may be detected and decoded by a remote viewer. When the remote viewer first detects the signal line it manifests itself as an influx of signal energy, which presents large gestalts of information (organized wholes perceived as more than the sum of their parts).

In his book, *The Reality of ESP: A Physicist's Proof of Psychic Abilities*, Russell Targ states, "I see a striking similarity between the nonlocal functioning of remote viewing in our SRI laboratory independent of distance and time—and the descriptions of EPR (nonlocal) optical experiments in the physics laboratory."

The Einstein–Podolsky–Rosen (EPR) paradox was a thought experiment conducted by Albert Einstein and his colleagues Boris Podolsky and Nathan Rosen. The experiment, which measured two particles, revealed that measuring one particle instantaneously changed the state of the second particle. According to EPR, a possible explanation for this was that even though they were separated, there was some interaction between the particles.

More recently, the discovery of unified field theories such as string theory have led to a greater understanding of the laws of nature. According to string theory, everything in the universe is comprised of tiny vibrating fundamental strings and each of these strings is identical.

According to theoretical physicist Michio Kaku:

In string theory, all particles are vibrations on a tiny rubber band; physics is the harmonies on the string;

chemistry is the melodies we play on vibrating strings; the universe is a symphony of strings, and the 'Mind of God' is cosmic music resonating in 11-dimensional hyperspace.

In addition, research in the field of neuroscience has revealed the existence of a "unified field of consciousness." This unified field of consciousness is distinct in that the observer, the observed, and the process of observation are one.

This new understanding about the nature of consciousness may indicate that quantum mechanics, the rules governing the physical world at the subatomic level, play an important role in consciousness. Physicist and author John Hagelin has claimed that consciousness comes from the higher dimensions, and, in fact, is the "ground of all being."

Exciting new research by some well-respected scientists shows that consciousness does not depend on the brain and may, in fact, survive the death of our bodies. The possibility of life after death is a long-debated topic; however, British physicist Sir Roger Penrose believes that he and his research team have found evidence that protein-based microtubules carry quantum information that is stored at a subatomic level. Penrose has stated, "If they're not revived, and the patient dies, it's possible that this quantum information can exist outside the body, perhaps indefinitely, as a soul."

Continuing research in the fields of quantum mechanics and consciousness research may soon provide compelling explanations for such phenomena as ghosts and hauntings.

What physicists call the *unified field*, the ancient Vedic texts known as the Upanishads call Brahman. Brahman is the supreme existence or absolute reality. Brahman is present in everything and appears to be synonymous with the unified field of physics. The field of quantum physics is now confirming what yogis have known for thousands of years, that everything is interconnected and we are all one. Because you and I are part of the same unified field, or Brahman, your consciousness is entangled not only with my consciousness but with everyone and everything.

Extensive studies over the past several decades have revealed to psi researchers the important role feedback and confidence play in the development of intuitive abilities. The neural pathways Ingo Swann spoke of are established by receiving feedback so that subjects might learn to associate certain mental states with accurate psychic information. Confidence also plays an important role in the development of these abilities, as it is necessary for the individual to trust the signals that they are receiving. Developing your confidence is one of the principle aims of this book.

It is an unfortunate fact that so many of us lose our ability to fully develop the natural gift of intuition because we have been conditioned not to trust our own instincts. We rarely enjoy the opportunity to receive accurate feedback regarding the signals we receive because we often lack the confidence in our own experience to share it with those around us. We habitually dismiss the information received through our "mental information processing grid" because we have been conditioned to do so, and therefore deny ourselves the opportunity to develop and master these abilities.

For many years I lacked the confidence that would allow me to fully tap into my own intuitive abilities because, like so many others, I had been conditioned to dismiss and disbelieve my own experiences. By the time I was a young adult, I had learned to pay little, if any, attention to my own inner voice. From a very young age I was told to dismiss insights, intuitions, and quiet knowings as mere imaginative fancy. Precognitive dreams were explained away as coincidence, and uneasy feelings about menacing strangers were regarded as the insecure fears of a shy child.

I suppose that it is hard to fault our parents and caregivers for this, as this conditioning is something that they most likely experienced from a young age as well. In fact, the impact that strong societal beliefs can have on behavior has been proven.

In 1951, Solomon Asch conducted laboratory experiments on conformity at Swarthmore College. In the experiment, groups of eight college students participated in a simple "perceptual" task in which all but one of the participants were actors, or "plants." The remaining participant was the true focus and subject of the study. The goal of the study was to learn how this subject would react to the behavior of the other participants.

In the study, participants were shown a card with a line on it and then shown a second card with lines of various lengths on them labeled "A," "B" and "C." The participants were then asked to identify which line on the second card matched the length of the line on the first card. Prior to the experiment, the plants had been instructed to give incorrect answers.

In 12 trials using different subjects it was found that 75 percent of the participants gave at least one incorrect answer during the trial in order to conform with the group.

Asch's study brings to light how willing we are to distrust our own experience in order to fit it with societal "norms." The results of these experiments make it is easy to see why we stop trusting our own inner voice and learn to accept the world only as it is presented to us, through the filter of societal beliefs.

It was not until I was out in the field, receiving confirmatory feedback in my work as a Reiki Master, yoga teacher, and massage therapist, as well as in my work as a paranormal researcher, that I began to truly trust that what I was experiencing was not only real, but accurate to a point well beyond chance.

Unless we re-learn to trust, and have confidence in our own inner experience, we cannot fully realize the benefits our natural abilities have to offer us, or be open to the opportunities and experiences that they seek to lead us to. In fact, confidence is so important that author, lecturer, and medical intuitive Caroline Myss insists that without a strong belief in ourselves we cannot truly master our intuitive ability. Myss has stated, "I firmly believe that intuitive or symbolic sight is not a gift but a skill—a skill based in self-esteem."

Remote viewing exercises can provide you with a wonderful opportunity to receive accurate feedback and, in so doing, build confidence. I often use the exercise below in my workshops on developing intuition and find it to be an accurate tool in assessing the way in which you access and receive information from the signal line. Because accuracy improves greatly when the viewer is in a relaxed state, be sure to practice this exercise in a stress-free environment, making sure to take the time to quiet your mind by gently breathing in and out from the diaphragm, which relaxes your body and stills your thoughts.

Remote viewing should be fun and not stressful. Don't get attached to the outcome! Better results are achieved when the viewer can achieve the relaxed brain wave states of alpha and theta, while anything that depresses the central nervous system (e.g., alcohol or antihistimines) has been proven to inhibit remote viewing capability.

Ginsing, ginko biloba, mugwort tea, and chocolate all have been shown to improve remote viewing abilities. Skills will improve with continued practice.

My Favorite Remote Viewing Exercise

You will need two friends to perform this exercise.

Have a friend tear out several different pictures from magazines and place each picture into a separate envelope.

Once this is done have this same friend label each envelope with a letter (A, B, C, etc.).

Have a second friend (who has not seen the photos) select one of the envelopes and give it to you.

Have a blank piece of paper and a pencil. Take several

deep breaths, clear your mind, and create the intention of establishing a connection with your "target." Once you have done this, allow your pencil to freely begin moving across your paper, creating lines or curves depending on how you feel. The key is to let your hand be relaxed and move freely across the page. Don't think about the process—just sketch the first thing that comes into your mind.

Do not rationalize as this creates what Ingo Swann termed Analytic Overlay, which is the analytic response of the viewer's mind to make sense of the information it receives.

Because it is a process of the viewer's analytic mind rather than the actual signal line, the Analytic Overlay interpretation is often wrong.

Next, notice any visual or sensory information, such as smells, tastes, and tactile data that enter your consciousness. Go with your first impressions and do not try to guess what the target may or may not be. As you record the sensory information you receive, let auditory cues enter your perception. Finally, allow the strongest of the data, the visual cues, come into your mind's eye.

Record your perceptions on the paper by making a series of simple drawings. As you draw your perceptions, try to connect them to the sensory information you obtained. Write down any descriptive information you may perceive, such as "it feels smooth," "cold," "rough," and so on.

Next, list any emotional responses by writing down the feelings you get from your perceptions. Perhaps you're noticing that you feel happy or anxious or excited.

> Once you have followed the steps above, open your envelope and compare it to the information on your paper.

The first time I tried this exercise, my first perceptions appeared to be very subtle, yet turned out to be quite accurate. As I tuned in to my target, my first impressions were of movement or of something flowing. Next, I got the sense of something soft and pink. Last, I experienced a pleasing floral scent that was quite strong and lasted for several seconds.

Upon opening my envelope, all my impressions made sense. The photo was an advertisement for women's perfume. In the photo, a beautiful young woman in a flowing pink gown reclined on a bed of pink flowers. The sensory input from this target had been so strong that I had made very few sketches except for wispy lines intended to convey the sense of flowing-ness of the gown that I had received.

I recommend not trying this exercise more than a couple of times in the same day. Allow yourself time to explore the subtleties of the experience and journal about it afterward. Most importantly, do not become attached to the outcome, but rather notice how the process works and feels for you and how you experience the signal line. In the long run, this information will be much more valuable to you.

Because everyone is different, the perceptions you receive from your target may be more visual than sensory. Some people receive data as literal and some receive it as metaphorical. The important thing is to not try to analyze or guess what your target might be as this will lead to Analytic Overlay. Positive feedback is the way in which neural pathways are established and confidence is created, so be sure to focus on what you got right about your target rather than be critical about what you missed.

As with all human abilities, each of us possesses a greater or lesser degree of talent in various sensing areas, but we are all born with a natural talent for accessing signal lines. However, how we detect the subtle waves of information contained within the signal is unique to each of us.

How these bits of information are processed depends on our own innate abilities. Some of us are born with an acute ability to see images that may come to us in flashes or play out like mini videos in our mind's eye. For others, the ability to feel or simply know things is more prevalent, and may manifest as a visceral "gut feeling" or externally as hairs literally standing on end (similar to what happens to dogs when their hackles go up).

With recognition and a little practice, anyone can learn how to tap into and strengthen their "mental information processing grid." We will explore how to determine the way in which you receive and interpret subtle bits of information from a signal line in a later chapter. Before we do, it is important to understand what the signal line is—energy.

3

HUMAN ENERGY SYSTEMS AND ENERGY AS INFORMATION

At our most elemental, we are not a chemical reaction, but an energetic charge. Human beings and all living things are a coalescence of energy in a field of energy connected to every other thing in the world.
Lynne McTaggart

It is time to stop invalidating experience that lies outside our Newtonian way of thinking and broaden our framework of reality.
Barbara Ann Brennan

The human body is a vibrant bioelectric organism that produces measurable electrical activity in the cells, neurons, and muscle tissues. For thousands of years ancient eastern cultures have recognized this electrical activity as the universal force that animates all living things. In China, it is called *qi* (pronounced chee); in India, it is referred to as *prana*; and in Japan it is called *ki*.

This universal force is your interface with the unified field and expands our awareness to energies beyond your physical body. Through this interface, you receive and interpret intuitive information. Thus, your ability to cultivate intuitive awareness is greatly improved with a basic understanding of human energy anatomy.

Eastern healing traditions have long understood that imbalances in the flow of energy can wreak havoc on our bodies and our minds. These traditions have not only been practiced for thousands of years, they have meticulously mapped the human energy system, creating practices such as acupuncture, yoga, Ayurveda and Reiki. These modalities have been practiced in the east with great effect and have made their way into western holistic healing over the past several decades.

I was first introduced to human energy anatomy more than 15 years ago when I began studying pranic healing (a form of energy healing in which practitioners direct prana to facilitate healing). Although the training I received in this technique was extensive, it wasn't until years later when I began practicing *asanas* (yoga postures) that I began to gain a better understanding of the way the human energy system feels, which makes sense as the *asanas* were designed to activate and balance the subtle energy body. I love practicing yoga, not only because of the way it makes my physical body feel, but also because of the energetic benefits I experience. It is only a matter of days should I get too busy to do my daily practice that I feel a significant drop in my energy. Conversely, after just a few days of committed practice I feel my energy at full levels again.

My subsequent Reiki studies and attunements opened an entirely new way of experiencing the human energy body. Whereas my yoga practice brought to me the experience of "feeling" my energy body, Reiki allowed me the alluring ability to *see* energy anatomy. My third Reiki attunement opened the world of energy in a way that I could have never imagined.

After the third attunement, I began to tune in to myself more clearly, increasing my awareness that I was becoming part of the natural way of things (think of the Tao, and the central image of flowing with the river). I found myself becoming *responsive* to the world around me rather than *reactive*. Rather than trying to override the almost compulsive need to *do* I was simply able to just *be*. As a result, my path began to unfold with less interference in front of me, and my personal and professional relationships improved tremendously.

From this awareness of the natural state of energy movement comes a way of being in the universe in which you are one with it all and begin to trust your intuitive heart. From this peaceful, balanced place of the intuitive heart you find yourself in a state of mind in which, rather than only noticing the clouds in the sky as you go about your day, you're able to understand that you are the clouds and the sky, and so much more.

Intuition is an ability that you already possess, so you don't have to possess an intricate understanding of human energy systems to cultivate Extraordinary Awareness. However, over the years I have found that my understanding of these energy systems has gone a long way toward helping me better understand how to integrate intuition into my daily life and also assist others who seek to do so as well. I have translated these experiences into the exercises you will find within these pages.

Below is an introduction to the basic concepts of the energetic body as understood by the traditional healing practices of Eastern cultures.

Chinese medicine

Chinese medicine encompasses a broad range of practices that have evolved over thousands of years and includes such modalities as herbal medicine, acupuncture, and acupressure. Integral to the practice of Chinese medicine is the belief that everything is connected. This principle applies to all systems and relates to the concept of qi, a continuous flux of dynamic energy that pervades everything. The terms yin and yang are used to describe the opposite qualities of qi and when yin and yang energies are in harmony with one another health and wellbeing are enjoyed.

In the ancient Chinese tradition of acupuncture, the flow of energy in the human body is intricately mapped out through a series of channels in the body, called *meridians*. Each meridian is a yin–yang pair, meaning each yin organ is paired with its corresponding yang organ. The concept of yin and yang is the foundation of diagnosis and treatment and although yin and yang are opposite energies they are, at the same time, interdependent. The female yin energy cannot exist without the male yang counterpart and vice versa. Yin literally means "dark side of the mountain" and represents cooler, less active energies, while yang means "sunny side of the mountain" and embodies warm, more active energies. Yin and yang are the positive and negative poles in the human electromagnetic system. In Chinese medicine, this relationship is expressed in the physical body and nothing is completely yin or yang. The symbol for yin and yang expresses this with a circle representing each in its counterpart.

Scientists at Seoul National University (SNU) recently confirmed the existence of meridians, which they referred to as the "primo-vascular system," which they say is a crucial part of the cardiovascular system.

The SNU scientists injected a special staining dye into acupuncture points to color the meridians and clearly see the meridian lines. The lines did not show up when the dye was injected at non-acupuncture point sites where there are no meridians.

Prior to this study, researchers used contrast Computed Tomography (CT) imaging with radiation on both non-acupuncture points and acupuncture points and discovered clear distinctions between the non-acupuncture point and acupuncture point anatomical structures. The study was published in the *Journal of Electron Spectroscopy and Related Phenomena*.

Ayurveda

Three thousand years ago sages of India developed arguably one of the world's most sophisticated health systems, Ayurveda. Ayurvedic medicine maps out the movement of the life force, or prana, through a series of 72,000 energy channels in the human body, called *nadis*. The word *nadi* comes from the Sanskrit root "nad" meaning "channel" or "stream." Prana enters the body through the Sushumna or central energy channel and travels the full length of the spinal cord. Two alternating channels of energy, the Ida and the Pingala, criss-cross along the Sushumna in a serpentine-like manner with the feminine Ida traveling along the left side of the central channel and the masculine Pingala moving along the right. These alternating channels travel upward from left to right and cross at seven major energy centers, called *chakras*. When these channels flow freely, we enjoy health and stamina; and when they become congested, our physical and mental health can become affected.

Fundamental to the Ayurvedic approach to wellness is the knowledge that each person has an Ayurvedic constitution (or *dosha*) that is specific to him or her. Doshic imbalances translate to health imbalances and Ayurveda addresses such energetic imbalances through a systematic approach that includes diet modifications, lifestyle adjustments, and herbal supplements. In addition, yoga, *pranayama* (breath techniques), meditation and *marma* or energetic pressure points are essential to addressing these imbalances.

Yoga and the subtle body

The 5,000-year-old practice of yoga was originally developed as a breath practice to focus the mind and enhance the flow of prana. The *asanas*, or physical postures, did not come about until much later when the Indian sage Patanjali codified the practice in his text *The Yoga Sutra*. Early yoga practices consisted mainly of *pranayama* that were designed to focus the mind and move energy through the body. According to yogic tradition, the subtle body or energy body is comprised of prana, which is distributed through the body through the *chakras*. When these centers are healthy and functioning properly they spin in a clock-wise motion, much like a wheel, which is what "chakra" means in Sanskrit.

On a physical level, the seven major chakras align with the body through nerve ganglia, correspond to glands and organs in the body, and are situated at various points along the spinal column. In addition, the chakras connect the physical body to the emotional and spiritual realms and correspond to patterns of behavior and specific "life themes." Symbolically, each chakra is represented by a lotus, which is depicted by a specific color and number of petals. Each of the chakras vibrate at different frequencies corresponding to sound vibrations. The sound vibrations produced by each chakra correspond to seven notes on the musical scale and are associated with "seed sounds," referred to as Bija Mantras. Chanting the Bija Mantras helps to bring chakras into alignment. When said aloud these mantras resonate with the energy of the associated chakra and bring it back to its proper vibrational frequency.

When the chakras are functioning properly, energy flows freely and the body is both physically and emotionally balanced. Factors such as our external environment and internal states can affect the vibrational flow of energy into and out of the chakras and when this occurs, one or more of these energy centers can become out of balance, resulting in the presence of either too much or too little energy. These imbalances can manifest physically as illness and disease, emotionally as depression, anger, or mania, and spiritually as patterns or themes that perpetually reoccur in our lives.

The seven major chakras from bottom to top are as follows:

The First Chakra
The Root, in Sanskrit: Muladara or "Root Support"

The Muladhara chakra is located at the base of the spine near the coccygeal plexus and is represented by a four-petaled lotus. Physically this chakra relates to the base of the spine, the legs, the feet, and the large intestine. Muladhara corresponds to the life themes of self-preservation and to basic needs such as food, water, shelter, and safety. The first chakra also establishes our connection to familial and cultural traditions that form our sense of identity. Patriotism, societal belief systems, and family traditions are all part of the energy circulating in the root chakra. This energy center literally represents our "roots" and is expressed when we share belief patterns with a large group of people. The Muladhara chakra is associated with the element of earth. Its color is red, its musical note is "C," and its seed sound is "Lam."

The Second Chakra
The Sacral, in Sanskrit: Svadhisthana or "Dwelling Place of the Self"

Svadhisthana is located above the pubic bone and below the navel in the location of the sacral ganglia. It sits two finger-widths above the Muladhara and is represented by a six-petaled lotus. Physically this chakra relates to the ovaries in women and the testes in men, and the adrenal glands, spleen, uterus, urinary, and circulatory system.

Svadhisthana corresponds to the life themes of sexuality, fertility, creativity and one-on-one relationships. The seeds of self-identity and personal boundaries lie within this energy center, as does our ability to bring creative ideas to fruition. Imbalances in this energy center might manifest as addiction, excessive emotional attachment to others, codependency or excessive neediness in relationships. Water is the element of Svadhisthana. Its color is orange, its musical note is "D," and its seed sound is "Vam."

The Third Chakra
The Solar Plexus, in Sanskrit: Manipura or "Lustrous Gem"

The 10-petaled Manipura is located in the middle of the abdomen behind the navel, near the lumbar ganglia and is also known as the navel center. Physically Manipura relates to the pancreas, stomach, liver, small intestine, and the digestive and endocrine systems. This chakra corresponds to the life themes of self-esteem, personal power, and identity. The energies in this chakra directly relate to self-respect, self-discipline, and strength of character. Imbalances in this energy center can manifest as lack of confidence, inability to make decisions, and giving our power over to others.

Manipura's element is fire. Its color is yellow, its musical note is "E," and its seed sound is "Ram."

The Fourth Chakra
The Heart, in Sanskrit: Anahata or "Unhurt, Unstruck, and Unbeaten"

The 12-petaled lotus of the Anahata chakra is located in the center of the chest at the cardiac plexus and is also referred to as the heart *center* for good reason; it is the center of the human energy system. Physically this chakra relates to the lungs, heart, pericardium, arms, and hands. Corresponding life themes are compassion, love, and healing. While the lower three chakras relate to our interactions with the physical world, the heart chakra is the bridge between the three lower chakras (physical) and the three higher (spiritual) chakras. The energies of the fourth chakra relate to our emotional development and our ability to express our emotions with ease. Imbalances may manifest as being overly critical of yourself and others, holding grudges, and an inability to give or receive love freely. The element of Anahata is air. Its color is green, its note is "F," and its corresponding seed sound is "Yam."

The Fifth Chakra
The Throat, in Sanskrit: Visuddha or "Purification"

The sixteen-petaled Visuddha chakra is located in the throat at the pharyngeal plexus and physically relates to the thyroid, parathyroid, voice box, ears, neck, and shoulders. Known as the purification center, the Vishuddha chakra gives voice to our spirit. Corresponding life themes include self-expression and communication, keeping our word, speaking and hearing the truth, and owning the consequences of our actions. When we lie to ourselves or to others we create imbalances in this center. Visuddha's element is sound. Its color is blue, its note is "G," and its corresponding seed sound is "Ham."

The Sixth Chakra
The Third Eye, in Sanskrit: Ajna or "To Perceive"

The third eye chakra is represented by a two-petaled lotus and is located just above the carotid plexus in the center of the forehead. Physically this chakra relates to the eyes, brain, and pituitary gland. The Ajna chakra corresponds to the themes of higher perception, wisdom,

inner awareness, self-reflection, imagination, and intuition.
Imbalances in this energy center manifest in the physical body as neurological disturbances, learning disabilities, coordination or balance issues, and vision problems, and emotionally as daydreaming and escapism. Ajna's element is light. Its color is indigo, its note is "A," and its seed sound is "OM."

The Seventh Chakra
The Crown, in Sanskrit: Sahasrara or "Thousand Fold"

The crown chakra is depicted as a thousand-petaled lotus located on the top of the head and represents our connection to the divine. Sahasrara governs the pineal gland and the central nervous system, and is the center of spirituality and enlightenment. It corresponds to learning how to experience the divine. Imbalances can manifest as feeling a lack of purpose, denying spirituality, or as an addiction to spirituality. Sahasrara's element is thought. Its color is white and its sound is silence.

While the descriptions above provide a basic overview of the chakras, an extensive understanding of the chakra system will serve you not only in the cultivation of Extraordinary Awareness but will also provide you with valuable insights into recurring life patterns and themes. Taking up your own yoga practice can go a long way toward an intricate understanding of your own energetic body, as can studying and reading as much as you can on the topic. Local yoga studios frequently provide classes and workshops about the chakra system, and I recommend taking advantage of such opportunities whenever they arise. Set the intention and send it out into the universe, and you will be surprised how quickly just the right thing manifests.

There is a plethora of excellent books about the chakras on the market. My favorite is *Wheels of Life: A User's Guide to the Chakra System*, by Anodea Judith. Revered as one of the foremost experts on the chakra system, Judith has written a book that is considered a classic in the field of energy work and takes a detailed look at the chakras through the lenses of physical anatomy, quantum physics and the Kabbalah. In addition, it features a section on how the seven chakras correspond to the steps for starting and completing any creative endeavor.

You can nurture and support your seven major energy centers in a variety of ways, such as diet, yoga, and meditation. The following meditation is a wonderful way to bring your awareness to your chakras and become familiar with the way in which you experience the energy in each center. As you practice this meditation, notice what you experience at each of the different energy centers. You may notice warmth, or a tingling sensation in the area you are focused on. You might notice coolness rather than warmth in a particular area, or you might not feel anything; everyone is different. You might notice that some areas are easier to concentrate on than others. When I find a chakra that is difficult for me to concentrate on, I make it a point to spend extra time focusing and bringing energy into that area. The more you practice this meditation, the more familiar you will become with your energy centers and the ways in which you experience them.

Chakra Meditation

Lie on your back with your legs and arms extended. Let your feet roll gently outward and allow your palms to rest comfortably, facing upward. Bring your awareness to your breath and take slow, deep breaths from the diaphragm as you allow yourself to gently settle into this position.

Now that you have taken several rounds of deep, cleansing breaths from the diaphragm and settled comfortably into this position, bring your awareness to your legs and visualize brilliant red light coming in through your nostrils as you inhale. Feel the warmth of the red light come into your nostrils and move to the area of your legs with each inhalation.

With each exhale feel the red light move down your legs and out through the bottoms of your feet. Inhale once again, drawing in the warmth of the red light and sending it down to your legs. On the exhale feel the energy move through the legs, to the feet and extend out from the bottoms of your feet like tree roots, creating for yourself strong healthy roots that will connect you to the earth. Continue visualizing red light coming in and moving through your legs and out through your feet in this way for a few moments before moving on.

Next, bring your awareness to the area between your navel and the top of your pubic bone. As you inhale, visualize brilliant orange light coming in through your nostrils and moving to the area between your belly button and your pubic bone. As you exhale see the orange light expand outside of your body like a small balloon. Inhale and feel the warmth of the orange light enter through your nostrils, exhale and see the orange light grow larger and expand to a sphere about the size of a grapefruit. Inhaling again, feel the warmth of the orange light as it enters your nostrils, and exhale the orange light into the growing sphere as it becomes the size of a volleyball. Continue inhaling and exhaling orange light in this manner and growing the orange sphere for several moments before moving on.

Bring your awareness now to the to the solar plexus chakra, the space in your body just beneath the bottom of your rib cage and just above your navel. Focus on this area right in the center of your body as you inhale brilliant warm sunshine in through your nostrils.

Next, feel the warm sunshine move down to the solar plexus chakra as you visualize this light expand like a balloon, move outside the body, and grow to the size of a grapefruit. Inhale once again, as you draw the warm sunshine in through the nostrils and send the bright yellow light to the solar plexus chakra. Continue expanding the light in this manner and growing the yellow sphere for several moments before moving on.

Next, bring your awareness to the center of your chest at your heart center. Inhale brilliant, emerald green light and feel it come in through your nostrils and move down to the center of your chest. See the green light expand and swirl at your heart center as you expand the balloon of green energy at your heart center and grow it to the size of a grapefruit. Inhale again, feeling the warmth of the green light as it enters your nostrils, and exhale the green light into the growing sphere as it becomes the size of a volleyball. Continue inhaling and exhaling in this manner, expanding the green sphere for several moments before moving on.

Bring your awareness next to you throat as you inhale cool, refreshing blue light. Draw this light down to the center of your throat and feel its energy as it swirls in the throat chakra and expands outside your body. Continue inhaling and exhaling in this manner, expanding the blue sphere of energy for several moments before you move upward to the center of your forehead.

Next, bring your awareness to your third eye chakra as you inhale purple light. Feel the purple light swirl and expand into a sphere of energy. Continue inhaling purple light and exhaling into the purple sphere of energy for several moments before focusing your attention upward to the crown of your head.

Finally, bring your awareness to the crown of your head and imagine that a strong beam of white light as wide as the top of your head enters through your crown as you inhale. Feel this light fill your entire body with each exhale. Inhale the warmth of the white light through the crown and feel the light expand larger and larger with each exhale. Continue inhaling and exhaling in this manner until you see the white light expand beyond your body to fill the entire room. After several moments bring your awareness once again to your crown chakra and imagine the beam of white light reduce to about half its size.

Continue to feel the warmth of the light as it enters and fills your body.

When you are ready, bring your awareness into your fingers and your toes and gently wiggle them and take a deep breath. With your next exhale roll on to your right side and gently move your right arm under your head for a pillow. Place your left hand, palm down, just in front of your heart center. Take a moment here to readjust and re-center.

Gently push yourself back up into a seated position. Once seated, take a few deep breaths, and then move on with your day.

Remember to take note in your Extraordinary Awareness journal of any sensations, thoughts, or feelings that you experience as you move your awareness to each of the seven energy centers. Be sure to take some time to write in your journal about what you experience each time you complete this practice. This writing activity will allow you time to process mentally what your body has experienced physically and energetically.

Having a strong and healthy energetic body is just as important as having a strong immune system, and it is important to spend time each day strengthening and protecting your energetic body.

Reiki

Reiki is a Japanese technique founded in the belief that a universal life force known as "ki" permeates and animates everything. The word Reiki (pronounced ray- key), has two parts. "Rei" means "universal," and "ki" means "energy." The purpose of Reiki is to restore balance to the energetic body, and to return the body to its natural frequency. During a Reiki session, the practitioner lightly places their hands over the recipient's body to facilitate the proper flow of ki through the body and restore energetic balance.

To become a Reiki practitioner, students are attuned to the specific frequency of Japanese symbols known as Kanji through a process performed by a Reiki Master.

Students are also trained in the human energy system to gain an understanding of what it means to bring the energetic body into balance. There are three levels of attunement that one can receive. A Reiki Master is someone who has undergone all three attunements and has taught Reiki and attuned others.

The Reiki attunement is an intense spiritual experience and many who receive the attunement report experiencing a noticeable increase in their natural intuitive abilities. Such was the case for me after I received my third Reiki attunement in 2010. Prior to my Level Three attunement, my experience with intuition had largely been limited to interactions with my inner voice in the forms of nudges and forceful shoves. After my Level III attunement, I noticed that experiences I had always had, but had dismissed as imagination, became so frequent and tangible that I was no longer able to dismiss them.

I liken a Reiki attunement to tuning an instrument. While you can certainly play a piano that is out of tune, the resulting music is much more clear and precise when the instrument is in tune. Our bodies are amazing instruments and once attuned to the higher frequencies of universal energies, our instruments resonate with clarity and precision.

The concept of a universal energy that pervades everything has been known to Eastern traditions for thousands of years. In the West, it has remained a subject of debate for the past several centuries.

Dr. Karl Ludwig von Reichenbach was one of the first to explore the topic through scientific exploration; he conducted hundreds of careful experiments on the vital energy that he termed the *Odic Force*. Like many intuitive trailblazers, von Reichenbach was questioned by his scientific peers who were steeped in Newtonian science.

At the time of von Reichenbach's research, Sir Isaac Newton's model of the universe as a massive machine comprised of solid objects was the prevailing model for understanding the workings of nature. This mechanistic view of the universe did not allow for the possibility of an unseen force, and held that all physical reactions have a physical cause. Ignoring his critics, von Reichenbach (trusting his intuition and Extraordinary Awareness!) spent 30 years experimenting with the Odic Force and found that it had many unique properties associated with polarity.

Von Reichenbach discovered what traditional Chinese medicine had said for thousands of years, that the force within the human body produces a polarity that renders the right side of the body a positive force and the left side of the body a negative one. This concept aligns with the description of yin and yang in Chinese medicine and with the Ida and Pingala *nadis* outlined in Ayurveda.

This universal life force, like all energy, has a unique signature that vibrates at a certain frequency. The human body, when healthy, resonates at a frequency between 62 Hz and 72 Hz. When this frequency drops, our immune system is compromised and a disease process is more apt to develop.

In the same way that cell phones, radios, and televisions carry information through wave frequencies, the human body also transmits information into the environment. We sense these waves of information and when we remember how to listen, we translate them into valuable information via our little inner voice (which, with practice, is no longer so little). Our bodies are constant receptors of energetic information, which we often feel physically or emotionally. When we experience a sense of caution or uneasiness in the presence of someone, the bioelectric sensors that Ingo Swann spoke of are detecting subtle bits of information being transmitted by the other person.

The HeartMath Institute (HMI) in California has good reason to believe that at the center of your intuitive ability is your heart. Since 1991, HMI has been conducting research on heart–brain communication, the heart's relationship to the body and how it affects our sense of connection to others. In fact, readings of interstitial heartbeats (the pauses between the beats of the heart) at the HMI have revealed that those pauses carry important information about our emotional state and show that our emotions actually modulate our heart signal. Research at HMI has also revealed that the heart generates the largest electromagnetic field in the body, shown by electrocardiogram (ECG) measurements to be about 60 times greater than that of brain waves.

These measurements of the heart's electromagnetic field reveal that we are like a radio station and a radio at the same time; we send and receive information with each heartbeat and in every moment.

HeartMath studies also show that this powerful electromagnetic field can be detected and measured several feet away from a person's body and between two individuals in close proximity. In one such study, two electrodes were placed into a petri dish of yogurt that was connected to a bioresponse meter. A human subject sat near the yogurt but was not connected to it by sensors. The subject was then asked to call to mind stressful events or memories. The yogurt's bioresponse meter registered a significant change each time the subject experienced an emotionally charged thought or memory. These studies clearly demonstrate that human emotions create a very real energetic field that radiates out from us in a measurable way and is detected by other living systems.

This is why we often get a "sense" that someone is in a foul mood and move away from them as they approach. Or, conversely, we say that someone is "radiating happiness" when they enter a room.

The more conscious you become of the quality of energy you are emanating, the better will be your personal relationships. Remember the story I told in a previous chapter about an early meeting between my two-year-old and my husband-to-be? When my son Jeremy requested a hug, he was tapping into the electromagnetic field of Joey's heart.

The emotion (Joey's anxiety) was detected, while the remedy (the hug) was intuited. As an intuitive and health practitioner, I find this understanding and awareness to be invaluable tool when working with clients.

Emotions have their own unique frequencies that are transmitted by the heart and influence the body. Research has shown that emotions like love, compassion, and gratitude register positive physiological affects on the body, and that our bodies function better in states of empathy, compassion, and love. Our thoughts and emotions affect our own bodies and living organisms within our proximity, and our world at large.

For over 50 years scientists have been observing devices called Random Number Generators. These devices electronically generate random numbers, the purpose of which is the equivalent of tossing a coin. There are 65 Random Number Generators throughout the world, and a half-century of studying these devices has revealed that in the presence of strong emotions, the generators cease being random and start generating organized sequences of numbers.

The largest measured event of this happening was during the September 11, 2001 attacks on the World Trade Center. Approximately *four hours before* the attacks began, a shift out of randomness and into organized number sequences was observed by the generators. This shift has been observed in over 250 events, such as tsunamis and other natural disasters. The odds against chance are a million to one that during those events the Random Number Generators would shift out of randomness.

Clearly, our emotions not only affect the generation of the numbers, but everything in the global environment.

In 1993 physicist John Hagelin conducted an experiment in Washington, DC to research the effects of meditation on crime. Four thousand volunteers came to the capital to collectively meditate to determine if the meditating group would reduce the crime rate over the course of the two-month study. The result was a 23 percent drop in the overall crime rate of the city. The following year Hagelin was awarded the Nobel Peace Prize.

What this means for us is something that ancient spiritual texts have testified for millennia—everything is connected and our separateness is merely an illusion. Understanding the energetic and electromagnetic properties of our bodies and how these properties work to send and carry information provides us with a strong foundation for understanding the inner voice mechanism of our intuitive ability.

The next step to understanding the workings of Extraordinary Awareness is an understanding of how the sending and receiving of this information is unique for everyone and manifests in different ways, depending on the individual's strengths.

4

THE INTUITIVE LIFE AND THE CLAIRS

The clairvoyant is simply a man who develops within himself the power to respond to another octave out of the stupendous gamut of possible vibrations, and so enables himself to see more of the world around him than those of more limited perception. **Charles Webster Leadbeater**

The Intuitive Life is the creative life. It is a life that allows us to apply what we know about the energetic world around us directly into creating fun and interesting lives rich with adventure and possibility.

Recently I was enjoying brunch with friends at a scenic waterside café. The conversation was cheerful and fun and our view of sailboats, paddle boarders, and the tiny island just across the channel contributed to our enjoyment. As I listened to the playful exchange between my friends, my gaze shifted to the way that the light played across the water. My attention was caught by a splash in the middle of the channel.

Excited at the possibility of catching a glimpse of a dolphin, my inner Magical Child focused attention to the area of the splash. When a dolphin failed to appear, I shifted my focus slightly and decided that the splash had been created by me, as a mermaid. Before I knew it, I found myself exploring the length of the channel in the company of dolphins. The sounds of the conversation faded away as I dove under the channel waters, playfully exploring with my dolphin friends.

Happy to have a new companion, one of the dolphins playfully approached me. I was amazed by the cool, soft smoothness of his skin. I grabbed hold of his dorsal fin and we dove under the water, parting a school of tiny colorful fish as we raced through the channel.

Before long, my dolphin friends swam out of the channel and into the open water. I decided to swim to the island beach and soak up some sun. As I lay on the sand enjoying the warm sunshine, a tiny crab crawled across my glistening mermaid flipper and I let out a giggle in response to the way his little crab feet tickled as they moved across my fin. As the crab waddled across the sand and out of sight a seagull landed right next to me. "Well, hello," I chirped.

My new companion stood staring at me, his head cocked to one side, and took a couple of steps in my direction. I loved the way his head bobbed with each step and as I sat there admiring him he spread his wings, opened his beak and said, "Isn't that right?"

"Hellooo? Tonya? Isn't that right?" From across the table my friend was trying to get my attention.

"I'm sorry...isn't what right?" I had returned to the pleasant company of my friends in the busy waterfront café.

And so it is with the Intuitive Life. It is a way of being where we can feel free to embrace our Magical Child and take advantage of unexpected opportunities to swim with dolphins, explore sparkling channels and hang out with seagulls all in the midst of a Sunday afternoon brunch with friends. We can seize these moments and treasure them for the gifts that they present to us. The gifts of gaining insights into ourselves and the way in which we interact with the world around us. Imagination and intuition both communicate in the language of symbols so it is important to take advantage of every opportunity to explore the meaning behind the symbols that our imaginations call forth.

Nothing is random. The symbols that manifest themselves through the playground of our imaginings come bearing messages and important lessons if we allow them to do so. When I explore the symbolic meanings associated with my mermaid persona I discover insights about myself as deep as the waters I imagine myself swimming in. There are also important messages to be gleaned by examining the symbolic meanings behind the companions who accompany me. Dolphins, crabs and seagulls each hold their own unique meanings.

Ignore what you might have been taught to believe about being mature, about being an adult, about being serious. Play! Treasures await in the depths of your imagination! If you have a hard time allowing yourself to daydream, perhaps it's because you were criticized when you were in school for doing it. But some of the greatest innovators of all time—Einstein, Jung, Tesla—made time for daydreaming. More than that, it was an essential part of all that they brought to the betterment of humankind. So, allow yourself to have fun seeking the treasures hidden in the depths of your imagination, and after you do, be sure to find time to write about your adventures in your Extraordinary Awareness journal. As you do, ask yourself these important questions:

What symbol am I?

What is my intention?

What are the symbols I find myself interacting with and what is it that I want to offer them?

Allowing yourself the opportunity to engage in this kind of creative daydreaming and exploring its meaning through journaling is an important part of strengthening the neural pathways that link your biosensors to your cognitive faculties. This kind of playful exploration is just one of the many things that makes the Intuitive Life so rich.

Understanding how our bodies send and receive information is another important step toward cultivating and trusting our Extraordinary Awareness. With this knowledge in hand we can explore the various ways in which we individually receive and interpret the signals we are receiving.

Most people are familiar with the term "clairvoyance"; however, many people are not aware that humans possess several "clair" senses. The word *clairvoyance* translates to "clear seeing" (*clair* means "clear" in French), and the term *clair senses* refers to the various types of intuitive sensitivity experienced. Clair refers to the ability to sense what is hidden from ordinary perception or awareness. We refer to the different ways the information comes to us as the clairs: clairaudience (hearing), clairvoyance (seeing), clairsentience (feeling), claircognizance (knowing), clairalience (smelling), and clairgustance (tasting). Everyone has some natural clair ability and many people find that one of their clair senses is more prevalent than the rest. With recognition and a little practice, anyone can learn how to tap into and strengthen their prevalent clair (or clairs). The exercises provided in this chapter will help you to identify your predominant clair and decide whether you are more visual, auditory, or kinesthetic.

The receiving and interpreting of these energetic signals varies for each of us according to our own innate abilities. Some of us experience images that come in flashes, or play out like a video in our mind's eye. Others detect these bits of information as words or phrases, or experience an intense knowing. Some of us might experience overwhelming feelings, such as happiness, fear, or anxiety, and others might experience all of the above. As you read through the descriptions of each of the clair senses, have your Extraordinary Awareness journal ready so that you can take time to reflect upon and journal about experiences that you have had that correlate to the various clairs. Be sure to also journal about what you experience when practicing each of the exercises provided below.

Clairvoyance

Clairvoyance means *clear seeing* and is the ability to perceive subtle bits of information as visual images. Often the images are not perceived with the physical eyes but are projected like a movie onto the screen of the mind's eye.

For me the images are projected onto the context of my surroundings. I take in the details of a room with my physical eyes, and as that information is being processed in the visual cortex of my brain, extrasensory impressions are being added to what I perceive. When a clairvoyant says, "I'm seeing such and such," we are often describing a psychic overlay on what we see with our physical eyes. The difference between these kinds of images and those of say, my swimming with dolphins, is that I generate dolphin images as part of my imaginative play, while my clairvoyant impressions appear without any thought or effort on my part and are quite often things that I, in even in my wildest imaginings, wouldn't think up.

Clairvoyance is one of the faculties that increased considerably for me after I had received my Reiki Level III attunement. Prior to my attunement, I would often experience quick flashes of images, but they were so faint and fleeting that I almost always dismissed them. Occasionally images would be perceived quite vividly and repeat several times and I would find myself confused by their meaning.

On occasion, I would experience an exception to this and would receive quite strong and vivid impressions. Once, while I was attending a workshop, a woman introduced herself and shook my hand. As she did, an image of her crying appeared very vividly in my mind's eye. This impression was accompanied by an overwhelming sense of grief and loss. Because impressions like this were so rare for me at the time, I was very confused by the image and had no idea what to make of it. As much as I wanted to offer support to the woman by giving her a warm embrace, I was too apprehensive and unsure to do so. I did contemplate it for the entirety of the workshop because every time I looked at the woman the impression returned.

Strong impressions such as this began to happen quite frequently after my Level III attunement and initially I found them just as confusing as I had before. One of the first Reiki sessions I had with a client after the Level III attunement served as an indicator of what was to come. As I was working on my client, the image of a small indigenous woman appeared next to me with such clarity that I could see every detail of her face and attire. She stood about four feet tall and wore a white top and a long, colorful skirt. Her tanned face was weathered with age and it was as if every deeply etched line in her face had a story all its own. Her dark eyes sparkled with joy and a tiny hint of mischief, and as she looked up at me and smiled I could see a glint of approval in her eyes. I sensed from her a deep wisdom and she reminded me of a tribal medicine woman.

This vision startled me and broke my concentration, and I told myself my mind was wandering and the woman was a figment of my imagination although I had made no effort whatsoever to "dream her up" as it were. (Keep in mind this was before I had learned to discern the difference between my own imagination and clairvoyant impressions.) As I tried to bring my focus back to my client, the woman chuckled, apparently amused at my attempt to dismiss her. I looked again and she was still there. As I moved around my client, administering Reiki to her stomach, legs, and feet, the woman followed me and clapped her hands with glee. Now I knew I was imagining her. Yet the more I tried to dismiss her, the more she chuckled and continued to show approving interest in how I was working on my client.

When I got to my client's feet, the woman said with a wide smile, "Tell her to drink elderberry tea!" Her eyes sparkled even brighter as she gave the direction. At the time, I knew nothing about elderberry tea and seemed to recall hearing that elderberries were poisonous. I soon found myself having a debate with a woman whom I completely believed to be a figment of my imagination.

"No," I thought. "I'm not telling her that. I don't know anything about elderberry tea, and anyway, you are a figment of my imagination." The woman chuckled and replied gently, "Tell her to drink elderberry tea, yes!" We went back and forth like this and all the while, the woman followed me around the table as I moved to apply Reiki to various areas of my client's body.

Finally, as the session came to a close, the image of the woman began to fade as she stood looking at me with a wide smile and that mischievous twinkle in her eye. I had insisted that I was not going to suggest elderberry tea to my client, and yet now I was curious. As I waited for my client to come out of the treatment room, I did a quick Internet search. As it turned out, not only is elderberry tea *not* poisonous, its benefits include reducing pain in the joints and inflammation in the body, issues that my client was chronically experiencing. When my client came out of the treatment room, I suggested she look into the benefits of elderberry tea and caught another quick glimpse of the joyful woman clapping her hands and chuckling at me lovingly.

Almost every subsequent Reiki session involved visitations similar to the one of the medicine woman, and eventually I began to take a chance and share my experiences with clients. Often when I would describe the visitors my clients' jaws would drop with disbelief as they shared that I had just described their grandmother, mother, or brother who had passed, but they felt was always near them. Even with the affirming feedback from my clients it took me quite some time to overcome a lifetime of conditioning and begin to accept that the beings I was encountering were not simply figments of my imagination.

Not only do my Reiki sessions now generally involve visitations from friendly guides and loved ones, I intentionally invite in any who wish to attend at the start of each session. In addition, I occasionally receive surprise visits from the loved ones of friends who've passed who wish me to convey messages, such as the time I encountered a woman I had never seen before standing in my bedroom who conveyed symbolic images to me that held very specific meaning for a friend of mine. I didn't know who the woman was at the time, but when I mentioned the visit to my friend the next day she was flabbergasted. I had just described her recently deceased best friend and the symbols her friend had shown me held special meaning for the two of them.

I feel very blessed to have the opportunity to meet people who have passed because were it not for the gift of clairvoyance, I would have not had the opportunity to meet them.

Exercises for Developing Clairvoyance

Clairvoyants are visual people. Because this clair sense is closely related to the faculty of imagination, practicing visualization can go a long way toward helping to develop your clairvoyant abilities.

A good way to practice this is by calling an image to mind and holding it there while you examine as many details as you can. The face of a loved one is always pleasurable, as are memories of favorite scenic places. Spend time each day with these kinds of images with the intention of observing more details each time.

Another fun way to practice requires the assistance of a friend. Find a quiet, comfortable place and have your friend sit across from you. Take a moment to clear your mind by bringing your focus to your breath. As you do so, have your friend call to mind the image of an object, such as a bicycle, a guitar or a volleyball. It doesn't matter what it is as long as your friend can create a clear image of it in their mind. Simple images work best in the beginning and can become more complicated as you progress.

Instruct your friend to incorporate any sensory information that might arise. For example, if your friend is visualizing a sailboat, she might also hear the sound of water, feel the wind on her face, or smell the salt air of the ocean.

After your friend has spent several moments visualizing in this way, set your intention to tune in to the object of your friend's focus. A good way to do this is by bringing your awareness to your third eye chakra. As you focus on the purple energy extending from the center of your forehead, see this energy extending and connecting with the third eye energies of your friend.

Keeping your mind clear, notice any images or sensory data that arise. Go with your first impressions—don't second-guess and don't try to analyze what comes. Information comes through differently for everyone, so take note of how it comes through for you.

Using the example of the sailboat, you might find that the first thing that arises for you is simply the triangular shape of the sails. Or, you might notice the sound of the water moving beneath the boat. Whatever impressions arise, present them to your friend in the following way:

"I see something triangular." Or, "I get the sensation of water moving."

Try not to ask questions, as this tends to quickly turn into a game of 20 Questions, a slippery slope that will soon lead to "analytic overlay," to borrow a remote viewing term, and thus ruin your chances of success. Just as with the remote viewing exercise, it is best not to practice this activity too many times in a row because after a while your analytic mind becomes bored and wants to become involved.

Once you have completed this exercise be sure to set an intention of breaking the energetic connection that you have made with your friend. I like to do this by visualizing scissors or hedge clippers cutting

> the energetic connection. Another way to break the connection is by sweeping your hands in front of your forehead a couple of times with the specific intention of breaking the connection.
>
> Old Maid cards are another fun way to practice developing clairvoyance. Shuffle the deck, select one card and place it, face down, in front of you. Similar to the remote viewing exercise from Chapter Two, take several deep breaths, clear your mind and create the intention of establishing a connection with the image on the card.
>
> Notice your perceptions and go with the first images that arise. After you turn the card over to compare, be sure to focus first on the similarities between your impressions and the image on the card. Journaling about this experience will provide you with valuable insight as to whether information comes literally or metaphorically.

Have fun with these exercises and don't get discouraged if your initial results are not what you'd hoped. It takes practice to clear you mind sufficiently to allow the images to come. Taking deep breaths from the diaphragm and allowing the breath to fully leave your body will help. And it is great for relaxing the body relieving stress!

Clairaudience

Clairaudience means *clear hearing* and is the perceiving of energetic information through internal or external hearing. A good example of this is if you've ever thought you've heard your name called yet you know there is nobody else around. As with clairvoyance, clairaudience is often perceived in a more internal way; however, it is not uncommon that information perceived by a clairaudient seems to come from an external source.

My earliest memories of clairaudient experiences are from when I was about five. I remember playing with my toys and hearing my name called from behind me or from another room, only to find that no one was there. This happened quite frequently and continued well into adulthood, when I began to have more clairvoyant experiences. In addition to hearing my name called I would frequently hear footsteps or voices from other parts of the house. Upon inspection, I would find that no one was there.

I am often asked questions about clairaudience. People frequently experience hearing things internally like songs and words, and are confused about where these sounds come from.

Joey and I do frequent investigations of the Webb Memorial Library, a haunted library in Morehead City, North Carolina. We are often joined by guest investigators. Although Joey never felt that he had much natural intuitive ability in terms of the clairs, he now realizes that his body receives subtle information through his auditory senses.

The first time this became apparent to him was during an investigation that took place in 2016. On this evening, we were joined by a family celebrating the 13th birthday of their son. The boy's parents and grandmother were with him, as well as the grandmother's boyfriend. At one point toward the end of our investigation, Joey kept hearing the name "George" in his mind, so much so that finally he had to ask the family if the name George meant anything to anyone. The boy's mother excitedly replied that George had been her father's name, and the birthday boy added that his main wish for the evening was to contact his grandfather.

During our investigations, we use a "ghost box" piece of equipment called the SB-11, which is a device that cycles through AM and FM frequencies without tuning in to them. The resulting wave frequencies create white noise through which intelligent communications are often received. Right after Joey mentioned that he was hearing the name George, we began to receive messages through the SB-11, which the family confirmed were expressions that George was known for. For example, he always replied in the affirmative to our questions by saying "10-4." When we asked the family if this was something George would say, they nodded and chuckled, sharing with us his fondness for CB radios. George also called out the name of the grandmother's new boyfriend, which clearly served to unsettle the new beau just a bit!

This experience went a long way toward helping Joey develop trust in words and phrases that come to him that previously he would have dismissed as imagination. If he had not trusted his intuition enough to ask the family about the name George, the communications may not have come through.

Exercise for Developing Clairaudience

Sit with a friend, take deep breaths and clear your mind. Have your friend call to mind a song or distinct sound.

Focus on establishing a connection through the third eye chakra as you did before, and also call to mind the blue energies of the throat chakra extending from the center of your neck and connecting with the blue energies of your friend's throat chakra. Remember that this chakra relates physically to the ears, so establishing this connection can help you tune into the auditory experience of your friend.

Allow the sound impressions to arise, and go with your first impulse without second- guessing or analyzing.

Share your impressions with your friend and be sure to journal about the details of your experience afterward. Break the energetic connection with your friend at the end of the exercise.

Clairsentience

Clairsentience means *clear feeling* and is the primary faculty of empaths. Empaths have the innate ability to feel and perceive what others are experiencing. If you're with your friend, and your friend has a headache, you might feel the headache as if it were your own. Recognizing what you are sensing empathically is important because otherwise you can spend your life experiencing the sudden onset of mysterious symptoms and never be aware of their cause.

Empaths are somewhat like psychic sponges, in that wherever they go they absorb the energies of their surroundings. They tend to become quickly overwhelmed and have a great deal of difficulty being in crowds. Energetically, it is like being in a room full of people who are all trying to talk to you at the same time, except that instead of being overwhelmed by voices, you are being bombarded with the emotional and physical experience of every person in the room.

For years before I learned about the clair senses, I was told by psychics and others that I was a "psychic sponge," and although I understood what they meant by this, I had no idea how powerful this clair faculty was until an experience I had one day in the grocery store. As I was walked past the dairy freezer my left knee buckled beneath me and was filled with an intense shooting pain. I had never had any kind of knee injury or pain, and this surprised me. I was at a loss to understand the cause. At that moment, the image of a man with an injured knee standing in the spot where I was standing popped into my mind. I saw the man quite clearly in my mind's eye and as I looked at him the pain in my knee increased. I realized that the pain did not belong to me, and suddenly the the pain went away. This was huge moment of understanding for me and since then, whenever I experience a pain or sensation that I have no explanation for, I ask myself if it is mine. I usually find that it is not, and upon asking the question, the sensation will vanish.

Interestingly, empaths do not just receive information from the people around them; they also pick up energetic information about places and objects. If an empath visits a location with a strong emotional imprint (a Civil War battleground is a good example of such a place), they immediately experience information about the emotions associated with that location.

Closely related to clairsentience is psychometry, the ability to sense something about an object simply by touching it. Objects hold energetic information and impressions, and this information is often picked up through clairsentience. Using an object for practicing and learning how this faculty works for you is a great way to develop this clair sense.

> ### Exercise for Developing Clairsentience
>
> You will need a friend to help you practice this exercise.
>
> Have your friend select a personal object that you know nothing about. The exercise works best if your friend selects an object that holds nostalgic or emotional meaning for them. Take a few moments to clear your mind, take a few deep breaths, then have your friend place the object in your hands.
>
> With your eyes closed, gently hold the object and wait for any sensations that may arise. You might experience feelings or sensations associated with the object such as visual impressions, or, you might hear names or words connected to the object. As impressions or sensations arise make a mental note of them, then clear your mind and wait a moment to see if you receive more information about the item.
>
> After a few moments share with your friend what you received; don't hold back. If something arose for you that seemed unlikely, share it, anyway. I can't tell you

> how many times I have dismissed information that seemed to me to make no sense, only to learn later that it made perfect sense to the other person.

If the impressions you receive do not seem to have a connection to the object, don't be discouraged! As with any new skill, it can take time to develop your ability to tune into your clair senses. In some cases, you might receive correct impressions that are connected to someone who owned the object before your friend, or to the person who made the item or gave it to your friend.

Claircognizance

Claircognizance means *clear knowing*. If you have ever had the experience in which you just suddenly "knew" something with great certainty, you have experienced this remarkable sensing system. If someone were to press you to explain how, you might reply, "I just know!"

Once I was staying at a hotel in a town with a history of paranormal activity. I had arrived late in the evening and was tired after a long day of travel. As I began to snuggle under the warmth of the down comforter I became overwhelmed with a strong urge to look under the bed. I thought it was silly and rolled over and tried to dismiss the urge. My attempts were useless. I could not get the urge to go away, and finally I gave in. I looked under the bed and to my dismay, retrieved an empty bottle of whiskey and several candy wrappers, apparently remnants from the previous occupant of the room. Once I put the items in the garbage can, I was able to rest.

I also experienced claircognizance the first time I met my friend Michelle. She and I met at a writer's event I was hosting. As we shook hands I was overcome with an instant knowing that this was someone I would really like. Over the next several months we got to know each other, and six years later Michelle is one of my closest friends and trusted advisors.

> **Exercise for Developing Claircognizance**
>
> For this exercise, you will go to a local used bookstore, flea market, or thrift store. Before you go, set an intention that you will find something that has meaning for you. Perhaps it is something that you have wanted for a long time and have not found, or it could be something that you have no idea about but once you find it, you will realize it has meaning or a message for you. As you enter the store take a deep breath and allow your intuition to lead you to a location. Trust your impulses as you feel yourself being pulled in one direction or another.
>
> You may find that you must listen to your body for the subtle impulses it is sending you. If you listen very carefully you will feel yourself pulled in a certain direction. Once you reach the right spot, scan the shelves until you find something that holds special meaning for you. The item might be synchronicitous (meaning that it seems coincidental) or it might be nostalgic; for example, you might have been remembering your grandmother and now here on the shelf in front of you is an item exactly like one that she had in her living room. Trust your intuition and listen to your inner voice, and you'll know what the right item is and what its special meaning is for you.

I experienced how this works for the first time when I visited a used bookstore to look for a book about the Greek myth of the Pleiades. It was a rather large bookstore and I was quite surprised to find that there were no books about the Pleiades in the mythology section. I kept feeling, however, a strong pull in my solar plexus to the cookbook section. I dismissed it at first because I was sure that the book I was looking for would not be found with the cookbooks. The impulse persisted and became so strong that finally I gave in and went over to the cookbook section, where, on a bottom shelf, I found the book I was looking for.

Used bookstores, thrift stores, and flea markets work well for this exercise because they provide a wide selection with low costs. It is much easier to let go and trust your instincts when you are not too attached to the outcome. I love sharing this exercise with my students because when I do, they come back with wonderful stories about the treasures that they found for themselves. I hold the same intention for you!

Clairalience

Clairalience is the ability to receive subtle bits of energetic information through the olfactory system. When this clair sense is engaged information is interpreted as a strong smell.

Joey and I experience clairalience almost every time we investigate the Webb Library. One of the residents of the Webb is a very distinguished doctor named Sanford Webb Thompson who had an office in the building in the early 1930s. During our first encounter with Dr. Thompson he shared his name with us through the SB-11. I was subsequently able to verify that Sanford Webb Thompson was one of the two original doctors who practiced in the building before it was converted to a library.

I always see Dr. Thompson in one of the library's first floor rooms, leaning against a mantle and smoking a pipe. I purposefully never say anything to our guest investigators about him until they have been in his room for several minutes. The reason for this is that guests will often go to the exact location in the room where I see Dr. Thompson and describe him, just as I see him, without my saying a word. Another common occurrence is that guests, upon entering the room, will frequently ask if anyone else smells cherry pipe tobacco. In another room, there was a persistent smell of peppermint near one chair and the smell of freshly cut wood elsewhere in the room. We spent considerable time looking for a physical explanation for each, and found none. The smells disappeared over the course of a few weeks, but not until several guest investigators noticed them.

The experience of clairalience has also been reported for centuries by those praying to saints and other religious figures who often experience the strong fragrance of roses. In Catholicism, the scent of roses is referred to as the "odor of sanctity" as it indicates the presence of a holy being.

The sense of smell is directly wired into our emotions through the limbic system. Well-trained actors employ a practice they call "sense memory" because smells can evoke deeply felt emotions within seconds. This is why certain smells have the ability to instantly transport you back in time to specific events, people and places, making smell one of our most powerful senses and an easily accessible clair ability.

Exercise for Developing Clairalience

Sit with a friend, take deep breaths, and clear your mind. Have your friend call to mind a pleasing, familiar scent, something you will recognize. (for example, their favorite perfume from high school is probably not the best choice).

Focus on establishing a connection through the third eye chakra. Allow the impressions of smell to arise, and go with your first impression without second-guessing or analyzing.

Share your impressions with your friend and include the details of your experience in your Extraordinary Awareness journal afterward. Remember to break the energetic connection with your friend at the end of the exercise.

Clairgustance

Clairgustance is the ability to perceive subtle information through gustatory perception, or gustation, which is the technical term for *tasting*. Clairgustance is similar to our normal sense of taste except that the items are not physically present. Encounters with Dr. Thompson provide another example for this clair sense. Occasionally, rather than smelling cherry pipe tobacco, some of our Webb guest investigators taste the tobacco. In the room I mentioned earlier, Webb investigators have also *tasted* the peppermint and cinnamon.

Exercise for Developing Clairgustance

Sit with a friend, take deep breaths and clear your mind. Have your friend call to mind a pleasing, familiar taste.

Focus on establishing a connection through the third eye chakra and allow any taste sensations to arise. Go with your first impressions.

Share your impressions with your friend and break the energetic connection before entering your experience in your Extraordinary Awareness journal.

With practice, anyone can learn how to tap into and strengthen their unique natural ability, or clair. For most us some clair senses are stronger than others, so as you practice the exercises don't get discouraged if you experience little or no success with some of the clair exercises. Clairalience and clairgustance are not among my strongest clair senses, and my success with the exercises for these abilities isn't always great. My results do improve the more I work with them. It's valuable for me to know that my natural ability lies with my other clair senses, and that first impressions for me will generally come through those faculties.

To determine which of the clairs is closest to your own natural ability, try the following visualization:

> ### Exercise for Identifying Clair Strengths
>
> Close your eyes and call to mind a significant life event or memory. Bring into your awareness all of the details about this event that you can, calling up any memories you have of how things looked, sounded, tasted, smelled, and felt. What stands out most in your memory? Take your time and journal about the details. Note which details were strongest for you:
>
> - *The sights associated with the memory*
> - *The sounds associated with the memory*
> - *The feelings associated with the memory*
> - *The smells associated with this memory*
> - *The tastes associated with this memory*
> - *The forgotten details that you recovered from the memory*
>
> Your answers to these questions, as well as your experiences while practicing the clair exercises, will help you to determine which clair abilities are strongest for you. The exercise will also demonstrate how powerful the senses are for recalling memories, and how strong the relationship is between our memories and our senses. It is no wonder that spirits will often communicate using a sound, a smell, or a taste!

Feedback is the most valuable tool for understanding and developing your clair abilities, so ask friends and family to provide it. If you suddenly develop a headache, ask someone in the room if they are suffering from a headache. If you meet someone and the image of a waterfall flashes through your mind out of nowhere, ask them if waterfalls mean anything to them. You'll be surprised at the answers you receive.

Remember the magic I promised as part of the Intuitive Life? The clair senses are only the beginning! The adventures you'll encounter as you delve into creative realms and are led by your intuitions hold within them infinite possibilities for having the full experience of the life you deserve!

5

STRANGE VISITATIONS FROM "GHOSTESSES" AND OTHER SPIRITS

We now have for the first time in the history of our species, compelling empirical evidence for belief in some form of personal survival after death.
Robert Almeder, Professor of Philosophy, Georgia State University

Like many other traits, clair senses tend to run in families. Ever since she was very small, my daughter Jolie has demonstrated considerable clairvoyant abilities. When she was four we visited a historic cemetery in Arkansas that had once been the location of a Civil War battle. As we stood reading the names on the headstones Jolie became very excited.

"Ghostesses!" she yelled, pointing in the direction of the trees bordering the cemetery. "Ghostesses are coming! They're soldiers! Do you hear the drums?" I heard the drums but couldn't see the soldiers, although I had no doubt about what Jolie was seeing.

"We have to go, the ghostesses are coming!" Evidently the soldiers were getting closer and Jolie felt our time was short before they overtook us. We left the cemetery and did our best to ease her fears without dismissing her experience, or telling her that it was her imagination. We did however explain to her that "ghostesses" (as she called them), were a natural part of our world and that while some people can easily see them, others cannot. Either way, we assured Jolie that the "ghostesses" could not hurt her. Since that day the affectionate name for ghosts in our family has been *ghostesses*, and I use it so often that I forget myself around strangers, who understandably have no idea what I am talking about. I have to chuckle every time this happens and take a few moments to share the story with them.

Living the Intuitive Life doesn't necessarily involve seeing or interacting with ghosts, but for some of us, seeing and interacting with them becomes a part of life whether we want it to or not. *Ghostessess* are a part of our natural world, and as physicist Sir Roger Penrose has discovered, may exist as protein-based microtubules that carry quantum information (as mentioned in Chapter Two). I prefer to simply think of them as people without bodies.

One of the most common questions I am asked by my clients is whether they can be visited by their deceased loves ones. Many of them have already had such an experience, and they are seeking validation, such as in the following:

> *My uncle was a heavy smoker, and ever since he passed a few months ago I keep smelling cigarette smoke. It was so strong at work the other day that my manager nearly fired me for smoking on the job!*
>
> *I could have sworn I heard my mother's voice the other day, which is impossible because she's been gone for years!*

My husband was always a practical joker. Since he's passed, certain personal objects go missing then reappear a day or two later. I can almost hear him laughing at me as I'm pulling up couch cushions in search of my car keys!

These are just a few of the experiences clients have shared with me over the years, and they are always hoping for the same thing. Validation. I assure them that not only are these things possible, they are quite common. I also encourage them to talk to their loved ones when they believe them to be present, a suggestion that is often met with surprise.

You mean they can hear me?!

Of course they can and they are clearly trying to get your attention, so the least you can do is say hello!

Have fun with these types of experiences when they occur. Talk to your loved ones and keep a record of these special visitations in your Extraordinary Awareness journal. You may discover that a pattern evolves. Perhaps your mother always visits at a certain special day or time of day, or when you're around certain people, or whenever you share her memory with someone else.

Although most people aren't frightened by visitations from their loved ones, they find visitations from anyone else from the other side unsettling and even scary. This, of course, has to do with our fear of the unknown. You know that your grandmother would never hurt you, while you know nothing about the *ghostess* responsible, for example, for the strange occurrences in your hundred-year-old farmhouse.

I didn't always think of spirits as people without bodies. In fact, my numerous encounters with them over the years proved to be just as scary and unsettling as you would imagine. My childhood was riddled with strange occurrences and unexplained phenomena, probably the most common of which was the sound of footsteps wandering the hallway and into my bedroom. On one such occasion, the footsteps could be heard moving around my room and then slowly making their way to my bedside, which then began to sink under the weight of my unseen visitor.

These types of experiences continued into adulthood, and I still have them to this day. In fact, in practically every house I have ever lived in, I have experienced late night visitations, unexplained occurrences, or both. While it may seem unusual for one person to have so many encounters with *ghostessess*, it really isn't. I think it is much like the character Alexander Leek says in one my favorite movies, *The Mothman Prophecies*: "You noticed them, and they noticed that you noticed them."

Because *ghostesses* are a natural part of our world, they are everywhere, and when they notice that I notice them, they seem to want to make sure that I *continue* to notice them.

From the time I was very young, I was told that I had a vivid imagination. This observation about me was accurate, but also overused. This is often the case for children whose parents do not have an explanation for the extraordinary experiences that their children relate to them. If disembodied footsteps wandered our hallways or my bedroom at night, or if I dreamt about something before it occurred, my parents would disregard it as "just an overactive imagination." And so it was for years, that rather than trust insights made available to me through my clair senses, I dismissed the information as "just my imagination."

On an almost nightly basis I would wake my parents to complain that I couldn't sleep in my own bed because someone was in my room. As you can imagine, my parents soon grew tired of having their sleep disrupted. Finally, my exasperated father put his foot down and forbade me from coming to their room. I was much too old, he said, for such nonsense. I knew that what I was experiencing was not just my imagination. And certainly not nonsense. Our family dog often jumped up and started barking when I heard footsteps or saw something flit across the hallway. The frustration of having these terrifying experiences so casually dismissed by my parents had a profound effect on me, so when my own children began to have similar experiences of their own, I took them seriously.

I was very fortunate to have a grandmother who not only recognized her intuitive abilities, but spent most of her adult life studying and mastering them. I was also very fortunate that she shared much of what she learned with me, schooling me in dreamwork, meditation, astral travel, automatic writing, and telepathy. I readily absorbed all that she taught me; however, I lacked the one fundamental necessity that would allow me to fully tap into my own natural abilities—a belief in myself.

My grandmother was an extraordinary woman. She traveled the countryside all by herself for many years, and spent the final days of her life living all alone in an isolated area of the Mogollon Rim of Arizona, with nothing around her for miles save cactus and coyotes. In addition to that, she was never afraid to be the authentic version of herself. She paid no attention to snickers received from those who disregarded her experiences as the ramblings of an eccentric old woman. She was in fact quite eccentric, with a wide range of interests. It has been my experience over the years, however, that all of the most intuitive people are eccentric.

Of all the qualities that I admired about my grandmother, what I loved the most was her unwavering commitment to be true to who she was. I have to admit, I have not been quite so brave. For many years I kept most of my experiences to myself out of fear that I would be regarded in the same light as my grandmother. As I gained confidence and grew braver, I learned that most people are quite open-minded, and accepted my experiences. Gradually, I became more comfortable with being open about my unique talents and experiences. The exercises and suggestions provided in this book are the same ones that have helped me on my path, and I hope they will do the same for you.

As I look back over my experiences, I especially remember one that happened when I was working alone in an old abandoned YMCA building in Fairmont, West Virginia. Joey and I had been given access to the building for a Halloween event that we were hosting for the town, and I spent an afternoon alone decorating inside the enormous building. Being alone inside a dark abandoned building was as creepy as you might imagine. As I entered the kitchen pantry, I heard a little voice behind me singing, "This Little Light of Mine." The voice had such an ethereal quality that I couldn't get it out of my mind, and to this day I can still hear it like it was yesterday. I shared this experience with a close friend of mine. She was delighted, and immediately saw a clear message for me. She still reminds me of it: "Stop hiding your light under a bushel and be who you are!"

The journey to being my authentic self has been a long one, and is still in process. However, the more I engage in the Intuitive Life, the closer I get. I was recently asked to give my impressions of a local art studio believed to be haunted. I later learned that the owner of the studio had shared with a mutual friend that she was awaiting the arrival of a medium, to which our friend replied, "You know Tonya Madia does that too don't you?" Joey later heard of this exchange and proudly informed me that the word was out about me. This is one more step in my journey to Authenticity.

Living the Intuitive Life and Authenticity go hand in hand and as you pursue one you become the other. Fearlessly, the way my grandmother did. As you begin your journey toward Authenticity, I encourage you to seek out the books and TED Talks of Brené Brown and Elizabeth Gilbert, as anyone on a journey to Authenticity will be inspired by their stories and by following their example. (TED stands for Technology, Entertainment and Design. TED is a non-profit organization that posts short, free talks online by leaders in these fields.)

One reason why so many of us lose our ability to be authentic and fully develop our natural clair abilities is that we have been conditioned not to trust ourselves. Throughout my childhood and for most of my adult life, I tried to convince myself that the late-night visitations and unexplained voices were simply figments of my imagination. No matter how hard I tried to dismiss them, I was always frightened. It didn't help that I had had many strange encounters in most of the homes I lived in as an adult.

The first of these was a house in Mesa, Arizona. In 1996, I moved in with my sons Daniel, 11, and Jeremy who had just turned two. The boys loved the sublevel family room because it was spacious and made a terrific playroom. I had nightmares the first night. From the start Daniel complained of an uneasy feeling and the sense that he was being watched, and Jeremy frequently pointed at what appeared to be nothing on the staircase and repeat the word "scary." One night not long after we had moved in, Daniel was downstairs in the family room playing a game on his computer when out of the corner of his eye he saw an old woman cross the room to the left of him.

A few nights later I was watching television in the living room, which was on the ground floor. The stairs leading down to the family room were just to the left of the sofa. I could hear Jeremy playing and murmuring to someone (whom I assumed was Daniel) at the bottom of the stairs. I didn't think much of it as I thought it was just part of whatever he and Daniel were playing. Suddenly I realized that Jeremy was saying, "Help me, help me." I ran downstairs to find Jeremy in a face down position, unable to move and barely able to make his plea for help. Daniel had been around the corner playing on his computer with his headphones on and hadn't heard Jeremy, nor had he been the one talking to Jeremy a few minutes before. I scooped Jeremy up and carried him up the stairs, and as I did he pointed to the top of the stairs and said "scary."

The final straw came one afternoon a few weeks later when Daniel was at school. Jeremy was taking a nap and I was in the bathroom getting ready for work. As I leaned toward the mirror to apply my mascara, I heard a sinister witch-like cackle so close to me that I felt the cold breath in my ear. This unsettled me so much that I ran into Jeremy's bedroom, picked him up and headed quickly down the stairs. I could feel us move through something I could not see. It was a sensation I had never experienced before or have since. It is hard to describe—it was as if the air was thicker, colder, and had substance in that particular spot. I took Jeremy to my parents and began making plans to move out of the house. Unfortunately, not everyone dealing with a malevolent presence in their home has the option to just leave. I didn't have the knowledge and experience that I do today; however, if I had, I would have been prepared to investigate to learn more about the presence, as well as how to clear the home of it.

Four uneventful years passed (as far as experiences with ghostesses that is), until I moved to New Jersey, into an apartment with Joey, the boys, and our daughter, Jolie. During our years at this apartment we experienced strange, and sometimes humorous, occurrences. (Finding humor in the Unknown when you can is essential when appropriate. It helps diminish the fear that comes with facing things we don't fully understand.)

We termed one such occurrence "the stinky old man" because of the unusual nature of the phenomenon. We would be sitting in the living room when out of nowhere a strange odor would manifest right next to us. The odor was distinctly that of a person who was in desperate need of a shower, and it would linger from a few minutes to a few hours and then vanish as quickly as it manifested. The odor would also move around the room, as if who, or whatever, it was attached to was moving around the room. Try as we might, we were never able to identify the cause of this. Fortunately, the phenomenon did not follow us when we moved out of the apartment.

Our daughter Jolie, who was a toddler at the time, would often point and ask who was walking down the hallway, when she and I were the only ones at home. Once while I was doing the dishes in the kitchen, Jolie came in from the living room and told me there was an old man on the couch. I ran into the living room and found the couch and the room empty. Another time while I was alone in the apartment washing dishes I felt something lightly tap my heels. I looked down to see Jolie's bouncy ball, which had been sitting quite still in front of the sofa the last I had seen it. For the ball to reach my feet, it would have had to have rolled several feet and turned two sharp corners.

As strange as our experiences at the apartment were, they paled in comparison to what awaited us at our next home. In 2004, we moved into a newly remodeled Cape Cod home in Tinton Falls, New Jersey. For the first time, the kids would each have their own room and a large yard to play in. We were all very excited. We were also at the start of a new business venture that held great promise for us. Unfortunately, it wasn't long before our excitement turned to fear. In fact, from the first day it seemed as if our time in that house would be overshadowed by bad experiences.

On the day we moved in, we learned that the master bedroom located in the finished basement had become badly flooded. We had to stay with family for several weeks so the water could be extracted and the carpet could be replaced. About a week after the work was complete and we were finally settling in, we noticed a subtle black film covering everything in the basement. We had no idea what it was. I would wipe it off only to find it again the next day. After a few days of this, the heating system for the home suddenly stopped working. We called a repairman to come and take a look.

I will never forget the look on the repairman's face when I opened the door upon his arrival. I thought it quite odd and a bit unsettling the way he seemed to glare at me as I said hello and thanked him for coming. His expression was so penetrating, in fact, that as I led him downstairs to the heating system I wondered if he was going to be ill-mannered and difficult to deal with.

As we descended the staircase, he asked me questions about things he couldn't have possibly known about. He asked about my grandmother Clara by name and told me she was with me; he asked who in the house was writing about knights and dragons, a reference to Joey's first novel, and went on to describe Joey, whom he'd never met. I often think about how silly I must have looked in that moment, as I stood there, my mouth agape with amazement as he went into more detail about my grandmother and relayed messages from her about conversations that had taken place between her and I years before her death.

The repairman (whom I will call Jack in the interest of privacy) went on to explain that he was a psychic medium and that he could see that, like my grandmother, I had the gift as well. Jack assured me that with some training and guidance I could become as proficient at "seeing" as he was and offered to come by the house on evenings and weekends to share his knowledge and experience. After inspecting the heating system, he found that there was nothing wrong with it except a missing filter; this was the reason for the black soot we were finding. (We had not checked the filter as we assumed it had been replaced as a matter of course prior to our moving in.) Jack's discovery may have saved us from carbon monoxide poisoning. The heater malfunction was so curious that I was confident that someone, perhaps my grandmother, had been looking out for us.

When Jack returned a few weeks later so much was going on in the house that I was more interested in having him do a reading on the house than starting my lessons in mediumship. As I led him room to room through the house, I shared what we had been experiencing.

We started in Jeremy's room, and I explained that Jeremy had been complaining that every night around 3 a.m. he would wake up to his stereo or ceiling fan coming on by itself. Once Jeremy had awakened at three and sat up to find not only his ceiling fan had turned on, but there were two people playing out on his television, which was turned off. The scene involved a man choking a young woman. Jeremy, who was 10 years old, was understandably shaken by this and left his room to go sleep on the sofa.

Next, I took Jack into Jolie's room. She was five and was also experiencing difficulty at night. Almost every night she would wake from terrible nightmares, something she had never experienced previously. We then spent some time in the hallway, where I shared that twice Jolie had witnessed a black mass floating toward the living room. We moved from the hallway into the living room, where I shared with Jack how we often experienced a sense of uneasiness accompanied by the feeling of being watched while in that room.

I also explained to him the troubles Joey and I were experiencing in the bedroom (nope, *not* those kinds of troubles)! Nearly every morning at 3 a.m. the telephone would ring, yet there was never anybody on the line. When we answered, we would often hear a series of clicks, beeps or static; sometimes there would be nothing except dead silence on the other end. Hippies that we were (and still are), we had only a beaded curtain serving as the doorway to our bedroom, and in those early morning hours after the phone calls, I would hear the beaded curtain swing as if someone had walked through it. I would lie painfully still beneath the covers.

I shared with Jack how footsteps would often be heard in conjunction with what sounded like a heavy ball bouncing across the floor in the third-floor bedroom when nobody was up there. I also noted that on several occasions I had heard the voices of children coming from the basement when I was the only one home.

Finally, I shared the encounters that both Joey and I had had in the house that, more than any of the other experiences, had left us with the desire to move our family to a safer, more peaceful home.

The first encounter occurred one afternoon as I was standing in front of the bedroom mirror applying makeup. Suddenly I noticed in the reflection a being standing behind me, its face peering just over my right shoulder. It was a humanoid figure dressed in a blue military jacket with yellow, fringed epaulettes. The body and uniform stood in juxtaposition to the face, which was that of a rather pink hog with tusks. As soon as the figure appeared in the mirror I shot around to look behind me and found no one there. The encounter was so odd and happened so quickly that I dismissed it, as I had become so accustomed to doing, and didn't mention it anyone.

Two days later the second encounter occurred. I was in the kitchen preparing dinner when Joey arrived home and headed down the staircase to our bedroom. Before he reached the bottom of the stairs I heard him let out the most unusual scream, and he quickly scrambled back up the stairs into the kitchen. What he described reminded me once again of my need to trust my experiences. Joey explained that as he neared the bottom of the staircase he looked down to find a humanoid creature with a hog's head waiting for him at the foot of the stairs.

After I finished relating these experiences, Jack offered a weak explanation for the events, stating that what we were experiencing was poltergeist activity and that it would soon pass. He then hastily stated his need to be somewhere else, assured me we had nothing to worry about—and I never heard from him again. I called him a few times to see if he might come and start sharing his knowledge with me, but my calls were never returned.

My grandmother had taught me enough about poltergeists to know that our experiences in that house did not fit the criteria for such activity. *Poltergeist* is German for "noisy ghost" and is a phenomenon that usually involves loud noises such as banging or knocking, and is frequently accompanied by objects moving about, often as if being thrown. The classic film by the same name begins with accurately portrayed poltergeist activity before devolving into a horror story.

A lot of research has been done regarding this phenomenon and it is largely believed to be more the result of human psychokinesis (the ability to affect matter with the mind) than of malevolent spirits. Poltergeist activity tends to be centered on pubescent teens (usually females), and psychical researchers theorize that the emotional and hormonal changes the child is undergoing produce a type of uncontrolled psychokinesis. A characteristic trait of poltergeist activity is that it often only occurs when the angsty teen is present. The activity tends to stop as abruptly as it begins.

The experiences we were having in the house were quite different than typical poltergeist activity. I was confident that Jack wasn't comfortable sharing what he had actually sensed in the house, and had made the choice to downplay the activity in an attempt to ease my concerns. That I never heard from him again convinced me that whatever it was that he sensed in the house had instilled in him the desire to never return.

Over the next few months the activity and events (both normal and paranormal) in the house continued to escalate in frequency, until one morning at 3 a.m. a valve on the hot water heater burst, flooding the basement for a second time. Although there was nothing paranormal about an old hot water heater failing, this was the final straw.

Immediately after that, Joey and I agreed that the kids and I should go stay with his parents until new living arrangements could be made for our family.

New arrangements were made, although they were temporary. Worn out by the financial and crowding challenges of living in New Jersey, we decided it was time to offer the kids a more relaxed pace of life. After looking at several potential states, we received through a close friend an opportunity to purchase three acres in the quiet West Virginia countryside.

Tucked into the hillside of a West Virginia hollow (or *holler* as the locals say, and we quickly adopted), our newly built home was the vision of the serene lifestyle we had envisioned for our family. Despite that everything seemed picture perfect, I found myself feeling very uneasy in the house from the start, especially in the master bedroom. Every time I was in that room I had the overwhelming sense that I was being watched.

Strange noises were a regular occurrence, particularly in Jolie's bedroom. Doors would often close by themselves. Lights would often appear in the house, starting small and growing in size before fading out of sight. Objects, usually belonging to Joey, would mysteriously disappear and reappear several hours or even days later. I would frequently wake in the middle of the night to the sound of banging against the back of the house.

One night I woke to see the figure of a little girl standing next to my bed. Not long after that I decided to take photos in the master bedroom when the strange feeling was present. In one of the photos, what appears to be the face of a young girl is seen peeking through the closet door, which was slightly ajar when I took the photo. No one else was present in the room when the photo was taken.

The mystery of the little girl was solved during an afternoon nap. As I slept, the young girl shared her story with me through a dream. In the dream, a blond pioneer girl of about 10 was hopelessly trying to find her way back to her homestead. After wandering through the woods for quite some time, she gave into her exhaustion and her fate, and lay down next to a large tree. I recognized the tree instantly as one of the very old trees on our property.

Several months later I was receiving a reading from a psychic who, without my mentioning her, brought up the little girl. The psychic told me that there was a little girl attached to me and that she had become quite fond of me. He also pointed out that the girl thought my husband was much too serious and she loved to play practical jokes on him by hiding items like his keys, to get him to lighten up a little.

Activity continued in cycles for the seven years that we lived in the "holler," and by the time we sold the house to move on to our next adventure we had become so accustomed to unusual occurrences that I was very matter-of-fact about them. My casual attitude about unusual phenomena was largely due to the research and investigations I was now undertaking. They say knowledge is power, and in my case, I found that to be absolutely the truth.

During our time spent living in West Virginia, I had the opportunity to become friends with several paranormal investigators. These friends taught me how to investigate the strange occurrences and overcome my fears about them. I came to understand that what we refer to as *para*normal activity is, in fact, just another manifestation of the normal condition of our planet.

Years of investigation have also led me to believe that certain places attract more activity than others. If you have ever lived in a haunted house or visited a haunted location, you may have wondered, "What is it about this particular place?" Many people believe that geography plays a big role in the paranormal phenomena experienced in a specific location. The Webb Memorial Library is a good example of this. Of all the places in which I have experienced strange phenomena, the Webb is by far the most active. I believe there are several reasons for this. One is the location of the building, which is situated just two blocks from the Morehead City waterfront. Many people have theorized that the salt water serves to amplify the electromagnetic field of the area. Add to that a large radio tower that sits directly across from the building.

Another reason is emotion, which is energy. I believe that emotional factors play a part in the level of activity experienced at the Webb as well. Native Morehead City resident Earle W. Webb Sr. built what is now the Webb Library in 1929, and for the first two years the building served as doctors' offices downstairs and a training facility for a textile factory upstairs. In 1934, the Webbs' only son, Earle W. Webb, Jr., contracted pneumonia and died. In honor of their son, Mr. and Mrs. Webb dedicated the building two years later as the Earle W. Webb Jr. Memorial Library and Civic Center. I can't imagine anything more emotionally devastating than suffering the loss of a child. As a standing tribute to the memory of their lost son, the Webb is infused with strong emotional energy, making it perhaps a beacon for lost souls.

Another reason for the library's paranormal activity is that the Webb stands directly across the street from the location of the original county hospital. During World War II the hospital provided treatment for hundreds of burn victims who were injured when German U-boats were sunk off the Morehead City coast. (We frequently receive communications in German through the SB-11 and have had German-speaking guest investigators have entire conversations with men we believe to be deceased German sailors. During a recent investigation, a psychic medium sensed a man whose foot had become stuck in a U-boat).

Finally, The Webb has been a private library since 1936, and every room is filled with antiques and books spanning nearly nine decades. Many of the books are from Earle Webb Sr.'s private collection and date back even earlier. Because objects can become imprinted with emotions, I believe that the collection of antiques in the library serve to further amplify the activity of the building. The history and activity associated with the Webb Memorial Library is so interesting that Joey and I started work on a book about this historic treasure.

Outside of the Webb Library, our new life in Beaufort, North Carolina continues to be one of noticing and being noticed. The town of Beaufort is very old and I encounter *ghostesses* here almost every day, both in our house and on the streets. Just two blocks from our house is a 300-year-old burial ground, and it is pretty common to hear footsteps following behind you as you pass by. I've also heard a woman crying and seen her wandering amongst the headstones and sprawling live oaks.

I am also aware of several businesses here in Beaufort that feature strange goings on. The activity includes items that are mysteriously moved; strange sounds; and the uneasy feeling of being watched. As I mentioned earlier, I have been asked by a few local business owners to use my clair abilities to help them get to the bottom of these occurrences. This has become one of my most favorite things about the Intuitive Life— being comfortable enough with my gifts that I can share them to help others.

I can't think of anything more authentic than that.

6

Developing Intuition in the Field

I believe in intuitions and inspirations... I sometimes feel that I am right. I do not know that I am. **Albert Einstein**

We started investigating the paranormal because we wanted to turn the tables on the paranormal investigating us. **Joey Madia**

I was once giving a presentation about being a Paranormal Investigator to a group of school kids. The presentation was part of an annual program called Pirates and Ghosts. If you ask me, a better name would be Pirates and *Ghostessses*, but no one did ask me. Never mind about that. Pirates and Ghosts is a wonderful program in which middle and high school kids are brought through various stations where they encounter pirates who talk to them about history, and teach them how to sword fight and fire a cannon. It's an air cannon, but it's still pretty cool.

Although the kids thoroughly enjoy learning how to be proper scallywags, one of the teachers recently wrote and requested that there be more ghosts in the Pirate and Ghost program. Eager to please, the coordinators of the program asked me if I would come and talk to the kids about being a paranormal investigator and share some of the experiences I've had during investigations. I now had yet another opportunity to let my *little light shine* and be my authentic self.

I admit, I was a little bit nervous about how middle and high school kids would react, but much to my surprise my presentation was received with enthusiasm and curiosity. That was, of course, after I convinced them that unlike the pirates they had encountered, I wasn't an actor. (Though to be fair, there just aren't a lot of job opportunities for pirates these days; the old-fashioned peg-legged variety, that is).

"I really am a paranormal investigator," I found myself assuring them. "I actually get paid to do this."

Once confident that I wasn't a performer who was there to pull their peg legs with made up ghost stories, I was able to share my experiences with them. My favorite part of presenting to the students was their questions and comments at the end. It was wonderful to be of help to kids who just needed someone to listen to their experiences without trying to rationalize, minimalize, or explain them away.

One of the greatest honors we have in living the Intuitive Life is in seizing opportunities to offer validation to the experience of others. The world is filled with skeptics and "poo-poo"-ers; what is needed are more listeners, believers, and supporters. If you wish to engage in the Intuitive Life, your challenge is simple. Be brave. Be open to possibilities, don't worry about needing to understand everything, but at the same time, try to understand what you can.

By the time I was 40, I decided that I was done being afraid of the dark and the things that go bump in the night. I was tired of not understanding my ongoing experiences with ghostesses. I had read several books about the experiences of others like me and decided rather than being passive in my experiences, I wanted to be active. I also decided to visit and investigate locations known for paranormal activity. It was during these investigations that I had the opportunity to start exploring my clair abilities and gradually overcome my fears.

For quite some time I have been intrigued by *The Mothman Prophecies*, a 1975 book by investigative journalist John Keel about a series of bizarre events that took place in the small town of Point Pleasant, West Virginia from November 1966 to the collapse of the town's Silver Bridge that spanned the Ohio River in December 1967. My fascination with the strange history of Point Pleasant put it at the top of the list of places I was eager to investigate. I began visiting in 2009 and continue to make at least a few trips there each year; I am never disappointed.

Joey and I had seen the movie adaptation of the book while we were still living in New Jersey and we loved it. It wasn't long after we moved into our new home in the holler that I discovered that the town of Point Pleasant was only a few hours away. Joey wasn't as excited about visiting as I was, but after a couple of years I got him to agree to a weekend trip.

We were instantly charmed by the small town, which sits at the convergence of the Ohio and Kanawha rivers. I was amazed by how the sleepy main street gave one the impression of being transported 40 years back in time. In the Mothman Museum, we were given a map to an area just north of the town known as the TNT area, where explosives were manufactured in a large plant during the Second World War. The area was of particular interest because it was the location of the first sighting of the creature that came to be called the "Mothman."

The story goes like this. One late November night in 1966 two young Point Pleasant couples were taking a cruise in the TNT area, where the plant was now in ruins and the area overgrown with brush. As they passed an old explosives facility they noticed two red lights in the shadows and stopped the car for closer inspection. When they discovered that the lights were the glowing red eyes of a large winged humanoid figure, they sped toward Route 62, the main road into town, where they claimed the creature chased them at speeds exceeding 100 miles per hour.

The teens raced to the police station and reported their experience. In the ensuing weeks and months, several other Point Pleasant residents had encounters with the creature, which local reporters dubbed "Mothman" (an odd homage to the Batman phenomena of the time). Mothman was accompanied by a plethora of interesting characters arriving as what author John Keel deemed "an ancient procession of the damned."

For the next 13 months, as if a portal to some unknown dimension had been opened, a series of otherworldly events plagued the sleepy West Virginia town. Strange lights appeared nightly over the rivers, streets, and farms of the town, and people came from miles away to witness them. Menacing men clad in plaid shirts materialized in bedrooms in the middle of the night and vanished as quickly as they appeared. Television sets frequently malfunctioned and phantom phone calls were a regular occurrence.

Sinister men in black suits interrogated and intimidated the witnesses to these events. An odd detail about these men was that their black attire and black vehicles were out of style, often by decades, and yet appeared to be brand new. The "Men in Black" also wore shoes with strangely thick soles and exhibited extremely odd mannerisms, such as a fascination with simple objects like ballpoint pens.

Whatever portal to the unknown was opened with the arrival of the Mothman was seemingly slammed shut with the collapse of the Silver Bridge on December 15, 1967. The bridge connected the sleepy Point Pleasant main street to Gallipolis, Ohio. Traffic stalled on the bridge, and in less than a minute, all three spans collapsed into the icy Ohio River. Forty-six souls were lost, leaving almost no one in the small town untouched by the disaster. Visitations from the strange entities abruptly ended after that cold December night, a well-deserved respite for the grieving town residents.

It is interesting to note that entities resembling Mothman have been seen all over the world, often just before a major disaster. For this reason, many cryptozoologists and paranormal researchers believe Mothman to be a messenger of doom. Still others wonder if it might be a manifestation of the intuition of the collective consciousness, similar to Random Number Generators becoming non-random, as I discussed in an earlier chapter.

Harbinger of doom or manifestation of the collective consciousness—either way the accounts of eyewitnesses recorded by John Keel in *The Mothman Prophecies* were as numerous as they were weird.

We left the Mothman Museum with our map in hand and decided to make a quick stop in a souvenir shop before we headed out to the TNT area. As we browsed, we struck up a conversation with the shop owner, Bob. Bob shared with us several photos that had been taken at the cement igloos located in the TNT area. Built during the Second World War to hide munitions, the igloos now sat abandoned, and almost all of them were empty. People have discovered that photos taken inside the abandoned igloos often produce strange anomalies. Bob asked us to be sure to share any anomalous photographs we might take there, and we promised that we would.

Bob felt that one reason for the activity in the TNT area was that it had been used by the Native Americans as a burial ground long before European settlers arrived. Out of respect for this possibility, we purchased some sage to leave as an offering while we were there. We left Bob's shop at 2:30 p.m. (this becomes important later) and made our way to Route 62, toward the TNT area.

Now a wildlife refuge, the area where the igloos were located was as beautiful and serene as one would expect—with one eerie, unexplainable difference. Although it was a beautiful sunny day, the secluded area, which should have been teeming with the sounds of wildlife, was noticeably quiet. As we walked along the path that led from the road to the igloos we had the overwhelming sensation of being watched. The feeling grew stronger as we reached the first igloo, and we hesitated at the large opening to the structure. We stepped inside for a moment to snap some photos and moved on.

As we made our way toward the second igloo, which was located a little farther down the path, Joey became extremely nauseous, a feeling that grew stronger the closer we got. Joey became so overwhelmed by nausea that we didn't even try to enter the second igloo. On many return trips Joey has gotten a reputation as being a kind of "human EMF meter" because his sensing systems are extremely attuned to changes in energy. Closing my eyes, I allowed my intuition to guide me where to place the sage. I was pulled to a nearby area where I placed the sage between two bushes and said a prayer. We made our way back to the car.

As we drove toward town we both commented on how strangely quiet and eerie the area had been; just as we were commenting on this, a gray figure leapt across the two-lane road in a single bound. We turned to each other and simultaneously asked, "Did you see that?" We each described seeing the same thing—a gray humanoid figure standing at the edge of a cornfield on the left-hand side of the road, taking a single leap across two lanes and landing on the edge of the cornfield on the right side of the road, then vanishing into thin air. It happened so quickly that if we hadn't turned to each other in disbelief, we might have dismissed it as imagination without saying anything.

Excited to share our sighting with Bob, we drove immediately to his shop. We were surprised to find the shop closed. We checked the time—it was after 5 p.m.! We could not account for the missing time. The drive to the TNT area took less than 10 minutes, we spent less than 20 minutes exploring a single path and a few igloos in the TNT area, and we drove straight back to town, which took another 10 minutes. The total amount of time our trip should have taken was 40 minutes, yet over two hours had now expired and we had no explanation for where the time had gone.

Bob was working in the back and noticed us standing at his shop door in complete confusion and let us in. After we shared our experience with him, he gave us the phone number of John and Tim Frick, well-known paranormal investigators who had been researching strange events in Point Pleasant for several years.

We contacted the Frick bothers when we returned home and arranged to meet them in Point Pleasant to retrace our steps and show them the location of our sighting. John and Tim had invited their friend Steve Ward, another long-time investigator of Point Pleasant and all things paranormal, to meet with us. Although we were unable to find an explanation for our sighting, a wonderful friendship arose from that meeting, and we began making frequent trips to the area to meet with our new friends and continue our investigations. We meet more friends with each new trip.

It's interesting to note that encounters with supernatural beings do not always signal danger and doom. Joey was interviewed for a possible guest spot on a television documentary about Point Pleasant, but the producers seemed disappointed that, by and large, we have only had positive encounters there.

I say "by and large" because, two years later, on a late November evening in 2011, our group of investigators, which included author and paranormal researcher Rosemary Ellen Guiley, was exploring the TNT area. After collecting our data, we headed out of the woods in the direction of our vehicles. As we approached the road, Rosemary and I became acutely aware of a large shadowy presence looming in the trees just to our left.

The ominous figure followed our group as we made our way back to the road, and vanished just as we emerged from the trees. Rosemary and I saw the figure clairvoyantly, projected onto the screen of our mind's eye. We both began to describe the exact same clairvoyant and energetic impressions of the being. This was an affirming experience for me as it went a long way toward building my confidence in my clair senses.

Affirming experiences such as the one I had with Rosemary are one of the many reasons why I enjoy investigating. Meeting new friends is certainly another.

Opportunities to be a listener, believer, and supporter abound when in the presence of others who are in search of the same answers as you. The inherent value of spending time with those who share similar experiences is clear when one considers the vast number of support groups in our society. I'm not suggesting that those who investigate the unexplained need a support group, but rather that connecting with others with similar experiences is invaluable.

Delving into the world of paranormal investigation offers so many opportunities for those seeking to pursue the Intuitive Life that it is certainly worth, well, investigating! Remember the Magical Child? I can't think of a better playground for the Magical Child than investigating unexplained events. To explore things that occur outside of our understanding requires exactly the kind of perception so natural to the Magical Child, a way of looking at things that may appear to be clouds, when in fact they are dragons.

That is not to say that we don't first take an Occam's razor approach. In other words, rule out the simplest explanations first. EMF meter spiking? Check to see if you're holding it near electronic equipment. Temperature gun detecting a significant drop? Check to see if it's aimed near an air conditioner vent. Once these things have been ruled out, the Magical Child is free to come out and apply her creative perspective, and in doing so will probably take notice of details that might have otherwise been missed. I have seen this happen time and time again when investigators look from a slightly different perspective.

One of my favorite examples of this is the time I described the ghost of a man in a flattering way. He was a handsome man and I described him as such. One of the investigators present noticed that every time I said something flattering, his EMF meter spiked. It was a playful observation that led to my being accused of "flirting" with the ghost. I guess inadvertently I was. Because the investigator trusted this playful observation, he was able to make the connection between my compliments and the EMF spikes.

When it comes to developing a relationship with your inner voice, I can't think of a more interesting way to do so than by using it in the field. Not only will your inner voice help you to tune into important information in your surroundings, as it did for Rosemary and me at the TNT area, it can also lead you to investigate areas you might have otherwise overlooked. The bookstore exercise for developing claircognizance is a great way to practice using your inner voice in the field. One of the first things I do when I arrive at a location is take a deep breath, tune in and allow my inner voice to pull me to various areas of the location. I am never disappointed by where it leads me. Inevitably I will receive strong clairvoyant input in those areas, find that other investigators are pulled to the same area, or both.

The human body is an amazing and delicate piece of equipment. I'd put it up against an EMF meter any day. Although Joey's "ability" in this area is strong, we have witnessed others all have the same feeling at the same time—nausea, lightheadedness, etc.—sometimes as many as 15 people at a time! Because feedback is an important part of learning to use any piece of equipment, having the accuracy of your inner voice corroborated by another (or 15 others!) is invaluable.

Using your intuition in the field also allows you the opportunity to engage all your clair senses. More often than not, you are investigating something unseen, and your clair senses become an invaluable addition to your efforts. This is also where all the practice you've had journaling in your Extraordinary Awareness journal will pay off. You will want to keep meticulous notes, making sure to document as much detail as you can. Be sure to include what you felt, heard, sensed, smelled, tasted, and simply *knew* during your investigation. Not only does this information go a long way toward proving details for your investigation, it serves to build your confidence and teaches you to trust in your abilities.

Since our initial trip to Point Pleasant, I have investigated several other interesting locations such as the Trans-Allegheny Lunatic Asylum (formerly Weston State Hospital), also in West Virginia, historic burial grounds, and several private homes and businesses. Each investigation offers a new opportunity to cultivate and explore my clair abilities. With each new experience, I learn to trust my initial perceptions, which are frequently corroborated when other clairvoyants are present.

Without this kind of validation and feedback from others, it would be easy for me to fall back into old habits of dismissing what I sense as imagination. That is why feedback is an essential part of cultivating one's intuitive ability. If you have the opportunity to participate in a paranormal investigation, particularly one in which an experienced clairvoyant will be present, it can go a long way toward boosting your confidence.

Another aspect of paranormal investigating that goes a long way toward increasing confidence is historical research. Sometimes I receive information through my clair senses that I can verify later through historical documents. I can't think of a better confirmation than seeing someone clairvoyantly and then later seeing an old photo of that person appearing exactly as you perceived them.

Also, if you ask me—and I guess you are by reading my book—historical research isn't only validating, it's a lot of fun. It's almost addicting. I have a hard time pulling myself away, and have spent many hours in many courthouses poring over historical documents.

Paranormal investigation also leads to an increase in synchronicities in your life. Many are connected to your investigation, but some are not. Either way, the more they happen, the more you will notice them. For example, just after I finished writing about my experiences in Point Pleasant, I looked up to see a moth resting on the wall directly across from me. Small synchronicity though it was, I had to smile. Then, a few hours later, as my editor was doing the final work on the chapter, a track from *The Mothman Prophecies* came on in his iTunes player.

Investigating the cause of unexplained occurrences has helped me overcome my fear of the unknown. The more experience I gain, the more confident I feel when encountering ghostesses. If you decide to try your hand at investigating, I recommend that you first ensure that your subtle energy body is strong and healthy. Practicing the chakra meditation provided in Chapter Three is a good way to strengthen your energy body; however, developing daily self-care habits that support not only your energy body but your spiritual growth is essential as well. These areas are the subject of the next chapter.

Ready?

7

CREATING A STRONG ENERGY BODY

When you inhale, you are taking the strength from God. When you exhale, it represents the service you are giving to the world. **B.K.S. Iyengar**

Meditation is good. One can attain a pure mind by one-pointedness and detachment. Meditate upon one point and you will know God. **Neem Karoli Baba**

Living the Intuitive Life begins with self-care. Your body is a highly sophisticated bioelectric instrument through which amazing things can flow, but only if it is properly nourished, rested, and cared for.

I've learned this the hard way. I've tried foregoing the obvious requirements of self-care, convincing myself that I don't have time for my daily meditation and yoga practices, eating food that does not support my health because I'm "in a rush," and ignoring the needs of my energy body in favor of running around like a headless chicken. It never works out, and thankfully, it never lasts for long.

Within a matter of weeks, I find myself disconnected and exhausted. Suddenly a light bulb appears in perfect tandem with that "aha!" moment. As I realize that my self- neglect is the cause of my discomfort and disconnection, I wonder how I got here *again*. And so it is—we do great for a while, then we stumble, then we get up again, do great for a while only to stumble again. It's all part of the journey, so don't be hard on yourself when you find that you've neglected your practice or succumbed to your cookie addiction. Simply acknowledge it when it happens and quietly and calmly correct your course. We are human and far from perfect. I promise you this is a lifelong process, so just commit to doing your best and have fun while you do!

Here are some tools to help you create a routine of self-care that will support and fine-tune the wonderful, sophisticated, intuitive instrument that is your body.

The following are techniques that I have practiced for many years. When practiced regularly, these techniques not only bring my body and mind into balance, they allow me to shift into that magical state of being that I like to call Extraordinary Awareness.

Grounding

We are electrical beings. Our bodies generate electricity, which is an important part of how they function. As the nervous system sends electrical signals to the brain, these electrical charges are delivered from cell to cell. This process allows for communication between our cells. The electrical signals in our bodies are responsible for controlling the rhythm of our heartbeat, the movement of blood and nerve impulses, and for keeping our circadian rhythms in order.

There is an exchange of energy between our bodies and the earth. When our feet make a connection with the earth, negative electrons are absorbed through the soles of our feet. The result is that we become synchronized with the negatively charged electrical potential of the earth. This process is known as "grounding."

Studies have revealed grounding to be a powerful antioxidant. The process of grounding has also been shown to relieve pain, reduce inflammation, and improve sleep. In addition, grounding improves the zeta potential (a property that is exhibited by particles in suspension) of blood, meaning that it improves the electrical exchange between red blood cells.

Making a connection with the earth is not only good for our bodies, it is important for supporting mental and emotional states as well.

Earth's natural rhythm, known as the Schuman resonances, has an inherent frequency of 7.8 Hz, the same frequency as human brainwave activity. Numerous studies have shown that there are important links between the Schumann resonances and cognitive functions, emotions, behavior, and memory.

Bringing your awareness to your breath and to your connection to the earth also serves to ground you firmly in the present moment. A wonderful way to make a physical connection with the earth is to walk barefoot in the grass or on the beach.

When you need the positive effects of grounding but are not able to get outdoors, you can ground your energetic body through visualization. The following exercise is an excellent tool for grounding, and I use it when making a connection with the earth is not available.

Grounding Visualization

Find a comfortable seated position, making sure that your feet are firmly connecting with the floor. Close your eyes and bring your awareness to your breath.

Breathing in and out, allow full deep breaths to enter through your nose. Allow your abdomen to relax and expand as the breath moves in. Allow the breath to move out slowly.

Bring your awareness to the tip of your tailbone and imagine roots growing outward from there. See the roots move down your legs, out through the bottoms of your feet and into the floor. Now visualize the roots as they move through the many layers of the floor and through the many layers of the earth until they finally reach the earth's core, where they connect with a bright yellow ball of energy.

Draw this energy up through your roots and feel its warmth as it moves up through your roots, into the bottoms of your feet, and up your legs. Continue drawing that warm energy up your spine and out through the crown of your head. Visualize this warm energy flowing from your crown like a fountain.

Now bring your awareness to the sun shining brightly in the sky. Draw this energy down through your crown and into your spine. Feel the warmth of the sun's energy as it moves down your spine, through your legs, into your roots, out through the bottom of your feet, and into the earth. See that energy connect with the yellow ball of energy at the center of the earth.

> See the alternating currents of energy moving up and down your spine. Bring the sun's energy down your spine on the inhale and send the earth's energy upward on the exhale.
>
> After several cycles of this, bring your awareness back to the fountain of energy you created at your crown. In your mind's eye, slow the flow of energy at your crown from an overflowing fountain to a steadily trickling water fountain (this serves to slow the flow of energy into the crown so that the chakra does not become overwhelmed).
>
> Take a moment to wiggle your fingers and toes before opening your eyes and reconnecting with your external surroundings.

In yoga, the practice of reconnecting your body to the earth is called taking your seat, and doing so assists in opening pathways that create the quality of consciousness that allow us to become fully present and centered.

Pranayama (Breath Practice)

The word *prana* is a Sanskrit word meaning "breath" or "life force"; *ayama* translates to "expansion" or "extension." Together the two words mean "breath extension." *Pranayama* is breath work that connects the mind, body, and spirit through the disciplined practice of controlling the breath.

The practice of pranayama directs the flow of energy in the body and is used to balance both emotions and the physical body. A daily practice of focused breath work is extremely beneficial for both the physical and energetic bodies.

There are many different techniques, ranging from simple to extremely challenging. However, the pranayama practice that I often recommend starting with is alternate nostril breathing.

The practice of alternate nostril breathing balances the left and right hemispheres of the brain, improves blood circulation, cleanses the *nadis* (energy channels), helps to balance the chakras (energy centers), and oxygenates the blood.

> ### Alternate Nostril Breathing Practice
>
> Sit in a comfortable seated position and allow the spine to lengthen and the shoulders to relax.
>
> With the thumb of the right hand, close the right nostril and inhale from the left nostril for a count of eight. Gently hold the breath in as you release the right nostril and close the left nostril with the pinky of your right hand.
>
> Exhale from the right nostril for a count of eight, hold for one count, then inhale through the right nostril for a count of eight.
>
> Release the left nostril and bring the thumb back to the right nostril as you inhale from the left nostril for a count of eight.
>
> (Beginners to this practice often get confused, so it is helpful to keep in mind that you will always inhale through the nostril that you just exhaled through, before switching sides).
>
> Each time you inhale and exhale through both nostrils is considered a round; continue the practice for several rounds, or as long as is comfortable. It is best not to

> overdo it when first starting this practice, and work your way up over time as your body becomes more accustomed to the increase in oxygen this practice provides.

Another pranayama technique is abdominal breathing. By the time we are adults, many of us have developed the habit of chest breathing. This method of breathing does not allow for full, proper breaths and therefore inhibits the amount of oxygen our bodies receive.

If you have ever watched a baby sleep, you have observed abdominal breathing. With each inhalation, a baby's belly expands and rises, and falls with each exhalation. Because we are so obsessed with sucking in our bellies, we develop the habit of breathing essentially backwards, drawing the abdomen in with each inhale and never allowing abdominal muscles to relax to make room for the expansion of the diaphragm.

Abdominal Breathing Practice

Lie down on your back and allow your body to relax. Allow your left arm to rest on the floor next to your body, and place your right hand on your belly.

With each inhale, allow your belly to rise and swell fully and feel your belly gently fall with each exhale.

Allow time for slow, deep breaths, inhaling for a count of 10 and exhaling for a count of 10. If possible, try to inhale and exhale through the nose rather than the mouth.

> If comfortable, increase the count of each inhale and exhale to achieve as full a breath as possible. The length of the exhalation should match the length of the inhalation. Continue this practice for several minutes, or as long as it is comfortable for you to do so.

Abdominal breathing is an excellent method of reducing stress and inducing relaxation. One reason for this is the effect that deep breathing has on the vagus nerve. The vagus nerve is the longest of the cranial nerves and controls the parasympathetic nervous system, which controls your relaxation response. Taking deep breaths causes the diaphragm to expand, stimulating the vagus nerve, which in turn activates the parasympathetic nervous system.

Finding time in each day to practice abdominal breathing will not only assist with stress reduction—it will provide you with quiet opportunities to explore the subtle messages your body might be trying to convey.

Breath Meditation

Meditation is the process of allowing your thoughts to flow freely without attaching yourself to them. Breath meditation is the practice of quieting the mind by bringing awareness to the breath. Breath is the bridge between the body and the mind, and it is said that the mind is the king of the body, but the breath is the king of the mind. If you have ever taken a deep breath and counted to 10, you have experienced the power of the breath to calm the mind.

Beginning a breath meditation practice can be as simple as finding a few quiet moments throughout your day in which you put everything else aside and bring your awareness to your breath. This practice can be initiated at any time and place, although I recommend setting aside a specific time and place each day, as beginning any new habit takes time and effort. By allocating a scheduled time and place, you provide yourself with the best possible chance for success.

I have had the most success with my meditation practice in the morning before I get out of bed. After waking, I take a few moments to position myself in a comfortable seated position and bring my awareness to my breath, allowing the breath to move in and out through my nose. On the inhale, I allow my lungs to fill fully by relaxing my abdomen, making room for my lungs and ribs to fully expand; as I exhale, I allow the air to move freely from my lungs without effort. As I am inhaling, I imagine that white light is entering and filling my lungs, and any tension is leaving my body with the exhale. I often see it being carried off on the wings of butterflies.

By spending a few minutes every morning cultivating this practice, you can bring calmness and increased mental clarity to your day. If you are new to meditation, I suggest starting with two to three minutes each day, and adding a minute or two each day, as you are able.

As you sit quietly with your awareness on your breath, you will probably notice that thoughts arise. This is to be expected—thoughts are the natural condition of the mind. Thinking is what the mind does, and meditation is not the process of stopping the thoughts but, rather, allowing the thoughts to flow without becoming attached to them. A wonderful visualization for this is to imagine your thoughts as leaves floating down a river. You simply acknowledge their presence and watch them as they pass by.

Another helpful tool is the practice of non-judgment. Judging is the trap that tangles us in our thoughts. Once the judgment arises, the mind follows behind it like a lost dog. It is easy to see how the process interferes with the goal of quieting the mind for tuning into subtle frequencies and cultivating your intuition.

The process of meditation is not about controlling our thoughts, but instead becoming the master of them so that when our puppy dog mind begins to wander off, we call it back to the present moment with our breath. Meditation, like any disciplined endeavor, takes time to cultivate, which is exactly why we call it a practice. When applied daily, the process becomes less challenging, and before long we can become the master our thoughts and quiet our minds to allow our inner voice the opportunity to share valuable information.

Mindfulness Meditation

For thousands of years the practice of meditation has been used to quiet the mind and promote inner peace. The physical benefits of meditation include lowered blood pressure, decreased tension-related pain, increased serotonin production, and a boost to the immune system. On a mental level, the benefits of meditation include increased mental focus and clarity, decreased anxiety and increased creativity, to name a few. The ability to quiet the mind to eliminate what I call "background noise" has a profound effect on one's ability to tune in and listen to your inner voice. Cultivating Extraordinary Awareness requires mastering the ability to tune out interference from both external and internal sources.

Intuition is a natural ability that we all possess. I truly believe that people who think they have no intuitive ability simply suffer from too much background noise. Their minds are clattering about and drowning out the signals that they are receiving from their inner voice and through their biosensors.

Mindfulness meditation, or *present moment awareness*, was the first meditation practice I learned, and it was explained to me like this: when you're cooking, you are fully aware that you are cooking, and when you're eating, you are fully aware that you are eating; nothing else is competing for your focus, just the task at hand, whatever it is.

Zen Master and spiritual leader Thich Nhat Hanh puts it this way: "Drink your tea slowly and reverently, as if it is the axis on which the world earth revolves—slowly, evenly, without rushing toward the future. Live the actual moment. Only this moment is life." Mindfulness has been practiced in Eastern traditions for thousands of years and has been shown to be so effective in reducing stress and stress-related illness and disease that it has been used in mainstream medicine for more than 30 years.

According to Dr. John Kabat Zinn, founding director of the Stress Reduction Clinic and the Center for Mindfulness in Medicine, mindfulness can be described as, "paying attention, on purpose, in the present moment, as if your life depended on it, non- judgmentally." The result of mindfulness is an awareness, a deep dimension of Extraordinary Awareness that has always been available to you. Mindfulness meditation provides you with a volume knob for your thoughts.

Like anything, mindfulness is a habit that takes time to cultivate, but by finding moments in each day when you can allow yourself to be fully present, you will begin to feel the benefits. Below is an easy meditation to begin your practice.

Mindfulness Practice

Find a comfortable seated position, close your eyes, and bring your awareness to your breath. Breathe in and out through your nose and allow full deep breaths to enter. Allow your abdomen to relax and expand as the breath moves in, and then allow the breath to move out slowly. Bring your awareness to your feet connecting with the floor, and without judging, notice how the floor feels against your feet and how your feet feel against the floor.

Now, bring your awareness to your legs and notice how they feel; really notice. Do you feel air moving across them? Are you noticing any other sensations in your legs? Notice any sensations without placing a value on them—they are not good or bad; they just are.

Continue observing as you bring your awareness up your spine, to your shoulders, down your arms, and into

> your fingers. Notice without judging. Next, slowly move your awareness up through your neck and into your head and face. Really notice every single sensation. What are you feeling... hearing... smelling?
>
> As you proceed, remember that everything is exactly as it should be in this perfect, present moment. Finally, bring your awareness back to your breath, wiggle your fingers and toes, and slowly open your eyes.

This meditation is a wonderful way to explore the practice of mindfulness meditation while getting in tune with your body.

Another wonderful way to experiment with a mindfulness practice is to bring your full attention to the present moment while you are eating. Bring your full attention to the appearance, smell, taste, and feel of your food. Chew everything very slowly into tiny pieces, savoring the way it tastes. Buddhist wisdom says that you should chew your food 40 times before swallowing it. Give that a try! Other thoughts will arise as you are eating, but as they do, return your full attention to your meal. It may take some time, but eventually mindful eating will become second nature.

Yoga

Yoga is an ancient practice believed to have originated in India approximately 5,000 years ago. Developed originally as a practice for enhanced meditation through breath awareness, the focus on *asanas*, or physical postures, did not come about until much later. *Yoga* is a Sanskrit word that means "to yoke, or bind" and is the discipline of creating a union between breath, body and mind to rediscover our true self. As we fully experience each pose, the patterning of consciousness subsides, allowing for Extraordinary Awareness to arise.

Although yoga began as a practice to enhance meditation, in the West what we refer to as yoga is actually hatha yoga. Hatha yoga focuses on a set of physical exercises designed to align the muscles, bones and chakras. The postures are also designed to open the many energy channels of the body (*nadis*)—especially the main channel, the *sushumna*—so that energy can flow freely.

Hatha is translated as *ha* meaning "sun" and *tha* meaning "moon" and refers to the balance of masculine and feminine aspects within all of us. This is the same as in the Chinese tradition of yin and Yang energies. Through the practice of hatha yoga, we develop a balance of strength and flexibility, learn to balance our efforts, and to surrender into each pose.

One of the most valuable things to be gained from a regular yoga practice is the ability to tune in and listen to our bodies. We live in a society obsessed with multitasking and as we go about our days attempting to achieve as much as we possibly can, we learn to ignore the signals—both subtle and profound—being sent to us by our bodies. The quiet practice of yoga allows you to tune into your body and receive the wealth of information it has to offer. I have experienced profound differences in the way my body feels both on and off the mat by tuning in and making subtle modifications to my position, alignment, or breath.

The body is the messenger through which the inner voice conveys warnings; for example, when the tiny muscles attached to hair follicles contract, causing hairs to stand on end. This reflex is initiated by the sympathetic nervous system, which is responsible for the fight-or-flight response. Cultivating Extraordinary Awareness requires that we notice and listen to the subtle feedback we receive in each moment from our bodies.

When teaching yoga, I frequently observe the extent to which we have been conditioned to ignore what our bodies are telling us, and I am always amazed. So many students insist on plowing their way into a pose, at the risk of injury, rather than taking the time to explore each pose gradually, quietly listen, and gently accept what their bodies are trying to tell them. I am equally amazed by the transformation I begin to see when the student listens to and accepts what their bodies are signaling. For some this comes naturally and for others, like myself, it comes with years of practice, quiet listening, and *noticing*, followed by noticing that you are noticing...

With so many different types of yoga available, choosing a class can be difficult, even intimidating, to those just starting out. Don't let yourself fall into the trap of using this as an excuse! It is hard to believe how often someone has complained to me, "I want to take a yoga class, but I just don't know which one to take!" Start with a beginner's class—it's the best way to learn the basic poses and become aware of your level of flexibility and endurance.

Some folks like to start their yoga practice at home with a book or a video. My first experience with yoga was with a video that I'd been given. Within five minutes I decided yoga was so boring that I never wanted to try it again. Years later I tried a class and was surprised by the difference. I found that not only was yoga *not* boring, it was amazing. Often, attempts to begin a yoga practice with a video are quickly aborted, as a video cannot offer you feedback or assist you with finding your way in a particular pose. There is also a lot to be gained energetically from being in a room filled with other yogis, which is lost with a video. So, while videos can be a great tool for those with some experience with the *asanas*, I find they are not always the best way to begin your yoga journey.

As a yoga teacher, I frequently hear potential students express concern that they are not "flexible enough" to do yoga. Rest assured, it is not necessary to be flexible to do yoga. Anyone can do yoga, and while there are some advanced poses in which experienced yogis can bend themselves into unbelievable positions, this is not the case with a basic yoga practice. Any yoga pose can be modified to meet and accommodate specific ability levels. I've heard it said by many yoga teachers that saying you're not "flexible enough" to do yoga is like saying you are too dirty to take a shower. Yoga is a practice that facilitates openness. This applies to our physical, emotional, and energetic bodies. We do yoga to help improve our flexibility, so thinking that you must be flexible to do yoga is very much like saying you have to be clean before you can bathe.

Once you have started your practice and become familiar with the basic poses and breathing techniques, you can explore different classes, teachers, and teaching styles. Everyone is different and different practices appeal to different people. Try as many types of classes as you can, and most importantly, have fun and never judge yourself. Accept where you are in your practice with no attachment to outcome. Simply be present and continue to practice. Sri K. Pattabhi Jois, founder of Ashtanga Yoga, was known for saying: "Do your practice and all is coming."

Children love yoga. I love teaching children's yoga classes because most children are not only very in tune with their bodies, they know how to have fun with yoga. They don't take it as seriously as many adults do. See your yoga practice as an opportunity for your inner Magical Child to come out and play. Have fun as you are learning and exploring the *asanas*. Learn to laugh at yourself! This will not only help you to connect with your body, but give you valuable insight into your mind as well.

My true yoga journey began with my closest and most influential spiritual mentor, Annette, who gently navigated me onto the path of mindfulness and self-awareness. I met Annette through letters from her, shortly after Joey and I were first married in 1997. She was Joey's aunt, older sister to his father and, in many ways, the heart, soul, and leader of his strong-willed Italian-American family. We still lived in Arizona at the time and Aunt Annette wrote from New Jersey, on peacock-adorned stationery, to introduce herself and welcome me to the family. She had a way of making me feel special before I ever had the honor of being in her presence.

Aunt Annette had an incredible way about her. Her presence both commanded my attention and created a quiet sense of centered calm. She taught, as all the great masters do, through the experience of day-to-day tasks, such as walking, cooking, and gardening, with an emphasis on present moment and intention.

She spoke with authority and taught me the most important thing I would ever learn: how to breathe and take my seat. She set me on the path to yoga long before it ever occurred to me to explore my first *asana* (or yoga video). Although she never once mentioned the word yoga, she provided me with the most effective tools for quieting the patterns of my mind I had ever been given—pranayama, mantra, and mindfulness meditation.

Another seven years would pass before I would ever step foot in a yoga class and discover *asana*, the tool that stilled the patterning of my consciousness and taught me to listen to my inner voice in a way that I never had, through honoring myself and my body. Over the years, my yoga practice has provided me with a means to learn the truth about myself and the world around me, the truth that we are all one and that our separateness is merely illusion.

Energy Conservation

The old saying, "where attention goes energy flows" is true. We begin each day with a finite amount of energy, and it is important to be careful about where we spend that energy. Caroline Myss explains it like a bank account: there is only so much in there; if you spend it unwisely, or too much all at once, soon you are overdrawn.

I recommend taking a few days to pay close attention to where you are expending your energy and record your observations in your Extraordinary Awareness journal. I'd be surprised if you we not surprised.

Every day we engage in seemingly benign activities that are, without our noticing, depleting our energy reserves. If we are taking relatively good care of ourselves and getting enough rest each night we wake each morning with replenished reserves of energy. It is important to invest that energy into thoughts, feelings, and activities that provide a return on your investment and support your energetic body rather than simply drain your body's energy account.

As you go through your day, listen to your body and pay close attention to activities that cause you to feel drained, anxious or depressed. Although it isn't always possible to avoid these types of situations, it is important to identify and avoid them when you can. Notice which activities or situations create the sensation of increased energy. After engaging in these activities, you will probably "feel" lighter and as if your mood has elevated. These kinds of activities support both your physical and energetic bodies rather than drain them. It's like depositing money into your account!

Spending time with people who understand and support you is another important way to boost your energetic bank account. If you have ever spent time with someone who requires so much of your attention and personal energy that you feel tired afterward, you have experienced first-hand how these individuals can drain your account.

These types of people are called psychic vampires, and for good reason. They literally "feed" on the energetic bodies of those around them. The most common way that they do is by turning almost every experience into an emotional drama. Everything that happens to them is the worst thing, and they constantly seek to pull you into this state of turmoil with them. It is important to establish strong boundaries with psychic vampires, or if possible, distance yourself from them entirely. If removing them from your life is not possible, resist getting pulled into their drama. Lending energy to their emotional states opens you to becoming an energetic smorgasbord for the psychic vampire. They are like the relative or friend who is always borrowing money from you without ever intending to pay it back.

Learning the Lingo

Messages conveyed to us through intuition often come to us in the form of archetypes and symbols. An important part of cultivating Extraordinary Awareness is becoming familiar with their meanings and interpretations. Educating yourself on dream interpretation, symbology, and prevalent myths and folktales is an excellent start.

Symbolic messages received through dreams are a great example of the way this works; however, if we look closely, we receive messages through archetypal symbols practically every day. As a matter of fact, we *are* an expression of many archetypal symbols, each interacting with the world of other living symbols around us. One of the most valuable tools for living the Intuitive Life that we possess is paying attention to the archetypal symbols expressing themselves through us and asking what these archetypes wish to offer to the living symbols we find ourselves interacting with.

This is the most fun and magical part of living the Intuitive Life. This practice, more than any other, brings me back to my childhood days of cloud-gazing and instantly shifts me into the quality of consciousness where wonder and magical potential reside. Wondrous things are continuously presenting themselves to you as guideposts for learning, loving, and growing.

An experience I had recently illustrates this brilliantly.

As I was driving to my massage studio one morning I looked up in the sky and noticed a bald eagle circling above. Thrilled with the opportunity to see this beautiful creature in flight, I could hardly contain my excitement, and continued to think about the eagle throughout the day.

As I was leaving my studio that evening, I noticed the front license plate on a truck that had backed into the parking space next to me. On the plate was the picture of a bald eagle and I chuckled softly at the reminder as I pulled away.

As I drove home, another pickup truck pulled in front of me. On the tailgate of the truck was a very ornate, custom painting of—you guessed it—a bald eagle. I smiled when I noticed that the rear widow of the truck was covered with a decal with yet another eagle. This made it quite apparent to me that a message was being conveyed to me through the symbolism of the eagle.

When animal symbols arise as messengers, I refer to a wonderful book by author, clairvoyant and shamanic teacher Ted Andrews, titled *Animal Speak*. I have used this book for years with great success. The message being brought to me by eagle that day was that of keen sight, rising above the material to see the spiritual, and the ability to see the overall pattern/big picture. At the time, I was allowing myself to get distracted by unimportant details in a situation that was taking my focus off long-term visions and the "big picture."

Eagle provided me with even further confirmation, along with a nod of approval the morning after I completed this chapter. As I re-read the chapter and made revisions, I found myself wondering, with so many similar experiences in my life, if my example of the eagle message was the one I wanted to use. I decided it was. Later that morning, as I was driving my daughter to her horse lesson, I looked up to see a bald eagle circling above my car once more. Although their populations are slowly increasing, bald eagles are still considered a threatened species, and I have only had the opportunity to see them in person three times in my life. Since two of those three times were related to the example I had chosen for this book, I took it as a beautiful confirmation of my selection.

Loved ones who have passed often reach out to us through dreams and symbolic messages. Aunt Annette had an affinity for peacocks, and I associated the qualities of that striking bird with her. On the day of her memorial service, I was, understandably consumed with grief and had already begun to miss her so much that I could barely breathe. At one point, I excused myself to go to the ladies room. As I opened the door to enter, I looked up to find an ornate painting of a peacock that reached from ceiling to floor. I smiled with the sudden understanding that she had not left, but would always be with me.

I will talk more about using archetypes and symbols to cultivate intuition in dreamwork in the next chapter. Mastering this language can help you tap into messages from your Extraordinary Awareness.

The tools listed above provide an excellent foundation for cultivating your natural intuitive abilities. Incorporating these tools into your daily life so that they become part of your Intuitive Life will go a long way toward helping you master your intuition. Exploring these practices on a daily basis will serve you well, but remember to laugh and be kind to yourself when you fall back into old habits. We call them practices for a reason; they are habits that require practice; lots and lots of practice.

Now, follow me to dreamland and the wonderful world of symbolic language!

8

DREAMWORK AND THE LANGUAGE OF SYMBOLS

I have less than six months to live. The Waponis believe they need a human sacrifice or their island is going to sink into the ocean. They have this mineral your father wants so he hired me to leap into their volcano. **Joe Banks**

The soul never thinks without an image. **Aristotle**

Dream: The Grain Field

I am driving down the interstate and there is a baby in the passenger seat next to me. Suddenly, I become very tired and pull into a huge grain field on the side of the road to rest. I take the baby and walk into the middle of the field as the tall grain waving in the wind surrounds us. As we stand there, I think about how nice it would be to have this much land, but I quickly realize how much work it would be to cut the grain.

A farmer comes down the hill in a very large combine. The combine is moving fast and I realize that it wouldn't be that hard to cut the grain with the right equipment. I realize the farmer is coming straight toward us so I draw the baby close and start to run.

Just as the farmer reaches us he stops to talk to people who have suddenly appeared in the field. As I get close to the road, I look at the baby, who is now in a stroller. I push the stroller to the road but am unable to locate the car. Realizing that pretending there is a car will work just as well, I mime putting the stroller in the trunk and putting the baby in the infant seat. I then get in the imaginary car and drive away.

After driving for a while, I notice two old women sitting at a campfire by the side of the road. I pull over and the baby and I join them. The women explain that they need help taking their horses to a nearby house. I offer to help them, and after the task is complete, we sit down to eat and I have a sense of satisfaction for a job well done.

One of the most fun and interesting ways our inner voice speaks to us is through symbols and messages relayed to us through dreams. The conscious mind often overlooks the details, messages, and emotions that it experiences during waking hours and stores them in the subconscious where they are offered to us again through the complexity of the dream narrative.

They say a picture is worth a thousand words and this certainly applies to the multilayered messages conveyed to us through dream symbols. The dream symbols above (which were taken from a dream in my 2011 dream journal) were powerful images that, when examined, provided me with useful insight into circumstances that I was navigating at the time.

For thousands of years, dreams were thought to be messages from the spirit realm, and ancient cultures looked to them for answers and guidance. It was understood that dreams could provide answers for complex problems, foretell the future, and offer valuable insights into the self.

Austrian neurologist Sigmund Freud, known as the founder of psychoanalysis, revolutionized the study of dreams when he began to analyze them to understand their relation to personality and pathology. Freud considered dreams to be "the royal road to the unconscious" and believed them to be the result of unconscious thoughts and repressed sexual impulses.

Swiss psychiatrist Carl Jung was an early supporter of Freud's work; however, he later rejected Freud's theories of dream interpretation because he believed dreams to be more than repressed sexual impulses. In 1912, Jung publicly criticized Freud's theories and his emphasis on infantile sexuality. As a result, the two parted ways and Jung went on to develop his own version of psychoanalytic theory. Jung stated that, "The dream is a little hidden door in the innermost and most secret recesses of the psyche."

Jung identified a universal language of symbols present in different cultures, which emerged from *archetypes* shared by the collective unconscious of the human race. According to Jung, these universal symbols show up in dreams, literature, art, and religion. The concept of archetypes dates back to the Greek philosopher Plato (424–347 BC) and his belief that pure mental forms were imprinted on the soul before it was born into the world.

Archetypes

Jung expanded on Plato's Theory of Forms and described archetypes as patterns of behavior within the human psyche. He said four are inherent in each of us: the shadow; anima/animus; persona; and self.

The Shadow

The shadow archetype represents the aspects of our personality that are hidden from our conscious mind, the dark aspects of our personality that we often try to reject. According to Jung, when the shadow appears as a character in dreams, it typically appears as the same sex as the dreamer. Identifying and assimilating our shadow is important because unless we do so, it continues to have a powerful influence over our conscious mind. All archetypes possess light and shadow aspects; the story of Dr. Jekyll and Mr. Hyde is an excellent illustration of what happens when we seek to suppress, rather than to assimilate, the shadow.

The Anima and Animus

Anima represents the feminine aspects of the male personality, while animus represents the male aspects of the female personality. the anima/animus bring balance to the psyche and are the psyche's expression of the yin and yang energies residing within each of us. The anima/animus also have shadow aspects. Such is the case with the Devouring Mother who smothers her children and stifles their growth (the shadow aspect of the anima). The shadow side of the animus is revealed when abuse of authority and hubris replace the benevolent qualities of a caring, masculine authoritative figure.

The Persona

The word *persona* is a Latin word that literally means "mask." It is how we present ourselves to the world through the various social masks that we wear and change according to who we are with and the situations we are in. The Persona serves to protect the ego by acting as a shield or barrier. Presenting our Persona to the world allows us to feel as if we can protect the ego from being so vulnerable.

The Self

The Self archetype represents the unification of the unconsciousness and consciousness of an individual and the psyche as a whole. Jung often represented the self as a circle with a dot in the center, the entire circle represented the self, while the dot represented the ego. According to Jung, the Self is created through a process known as individuation. Through the process of individuation, the personal and collective unconscious are brought forward into the consciousness.

Examining dreams and participating in active imagination can help to facilitate this process.

In addition, other archetypes can play major roles in our lives. Here are some of the most common:

The Wise Old Man

The Wise Old Man represents the kind and wise elder who uses his knowledge to offer mystical guidance to remind us of who we truly are so that we can achieve our true potential. The Wise Old Man archetype is such a central part of human consciousness that he is a staple of storytelling and a classic literary figure. Obi-Wan Kenobi of the *Star Wars* saga is the perfect embodiment of The Wise Old Man archetype. A source of instinctive and age-old wisdom, this archetype often appears in dreams during periods of transition and self-transformation.

Over the years many authors and psychologists have sought to expand on archetypal symbols. I have always found the work of author Caroline Myss to be extraordinarily relevant and accessible. Myss has spent the past several decades expanding on the work of Carl Jung, writing and teaching about how to understand and engage with the archetypal patterns within.

In her book *Sacred Contracts: Awakening Your Divine Potential*, Myss outlines four universal archetypes inherent in each of us:

The Child

We all possess an inner child, an innocent part of our psyche that balances our serious adult nature with a sense of wonder and playfulness. According to Myss, aspects of the Child archetype include the Divine Child, the Wounded Child, and the Nature Child (to name a few). Peter Pan is an archetypal expression of the Eternal Child, also known as the *puer aeternus* or "eternal boy," and Lewis Carroll's *Alice in Wonderland* is an expression of the Magical Child. The exercises provided in this book are intended to help you cultivate Extraordinary Awareness and provide an outlet for your inner Magical Child, who understands the value of imagination and believes that anything is possible.

The Victim

The Victim archetype can prevent us from playing the victim and help us to recognize our own tendencies to victimize others. The shadow aspect of the Victim seeks to shift the responsibility of their circumstances on to others. My favorite example of an exploration of the shadow Victim is the 1990 movie *Joe Versus the Volcano*.

In the movie, Joe (played by Tom Hanks) is a hypochondriac who believes himself to be a passenger in his own life. After being falsely diagnosed with an incurable disease described as a "brain cloud," Joe quits his demoralizing job and accepts an offer to embark on an exciting journey that must end with him sacrificing himself to a volcano. His journey to the volcano is a witty exploration of several of the archetypal patterns and culminates with Joe and his newfound love Patricia (played by Meg Ryan) jumping fearlessly into the volcano, which promptly blows them out and into the safety of the ocean.

Once in the ocean, Joe does not share Patricia's excitement about their good fortune, but reveals to her that he has the fatal "brain cloud" illness, but never got a second medical opinion. Patricia asks, "You were diagnosed with something called a brain cloud and didn't ask for a second opinion?"

We then discover that the doctor who gave Joe the diagnosis works for Patricia's father (the man who hired Joe to jump into the volcano). Joe, realizing that he's been manipulated says, "My whole life I've been a victim. I've been a dupe. A pawn."

Patricia points out to Joe that, rather than having a fatal illness, he now has his whole life ahead of him. Joe agrees but quickly turns his attention to their current predicament of being on a raft in the middle of the ocean. Patricia responds, "It's always going to be something with you Joe, isn't it?"

Yes Patricia, for the shadow Victim it is always going to be something.

The Prostitute

The old adage "Everyone has a price" is at the heart of the Prostitute archetype, and at one time or another each of us has probably compromised core values in exchange for something we desired, whether material or emotional. Light aspects of the Prostitute archetype can help us navigate the world without compromising our beliefs, while the shadow Prostitute places material gain and security above self-actualization. The character of Faust, who sells his soul for knowledge, is a good example of this archetype.

The Saboteur

Within each of us lies the unique ability to get in our own way and destroy efforts that would otherwise lead us to success and happiness. The Saboteur's efforts to undermine us arise from unconscious beliefs that we are not enough and therefore not deserving of happiness. We can learn much from the Saboteur when we are willing to be completely honest with ourselves and recognize situations in which we sabotage our own efforts. Refusing to take an honest look at these patterns can manifest as jealousy, bitterness, and a desire to undermine the success of others. One of the Founding Fathers, Alexander Hamilton—who has enjoyed a resurgence of popularity due to the hit Broadway musical—is a real-life example of this archetype. His inability to move past his orphan, immigrant childhood resulted in him sabotaging himself throughout and at the peak of his career. It is interesting how many politicians seem to exhibit the traits of the Saboteur.

In her years of extensive work on archetypes, Caroline Myss has come to the conclusion that each of us has been encoded with a set of 12 primary archetypes, four of which are the survival archetypes mentioned above. Detailed descriptions of more than 70 archetypes can be found on her website, www.myss.com. Exploring these patterns through Myss' work has been an invaluable part of my personal growth and my ability to live an Intuitive Life. I recommend her books and workshops to anyone seeking a greater understanding of themselves and their unique intuitive abilities.

Exploration of our dreams can provide us with powerful insights into ourselves and our lives. It is no wonder that throughout history humans have found themselves so fascinated with them. Dream dictionaries provide general information about symbolic meanings, but do not offer the most accurate insight into the meaning of your dreams. The reason for this is very simple: life experience.

For example, a dream dictionary might say that a dream of a dog signifies loyalty, generosity, protection, and fidelity, but someone who has had a traumatic experience with a dog will make negative associations. The way that *I* feel about a dog may not be how *you* feel about a dog, and for this reason, no one can provide a more accurate interpretation of your dreams than you.

Familiarizing yourself with the many archetypal patterns of the psyche will help you evaluate and understand your dreams. Another important approach is to identify what symbol represents you in the dream landscape. This was suggested to me by a close friend and mentor, and I have found that it reveals surprising details contained within dream messages. As you examine your dream ask yourself:

What living symbol do I represent in this dream?

What do I want to offer to the other living symbols in my dream?

What am I seeking from the other living symbols in my dream?

The dream landscape represents aspects of the psyche, so an extensive exploration of the landscape can provide you with valuable insights, especially concerning the multilayered meanings in dreams. As you recall and journal your dreams, include as much detail about the surrounding landscape as possible.

The subconscious is an extremely efficient storyteller and can effectively convey information that applies to many issues in one swift dream. In my 2011 dream that opens this chapter, the dream landscape of the grain field provided insight into aspects of my psyche at the time, as well as insight that the endeavor I was undertaking required hard work and the "right equipment." The symbol of the combine represented the skills that would be required of me, such as moving fast and staying sharp.

Asking myself which living symbol I represented in this dream led me to a unique understanding. I realized that the symbol was the grain field—I was not *in* the grain field, I was the grain field. This revealed to me that I felt like the grain waving in the wind; I was standing tall while remaining movable. The baby in my dream represented an aspect of my own Child archetype and my new venture, which would require a great deal of nurturing and protection.

The farmer chasing me with the combine revealed my Saboteur and provided a warning that stopping to dilly dally (illustrated by the farmer idly chatting with the people in the field) would slow me down and prevent me from reaching my goals. My Victim archetype was revealed when I realized that my car was gone; however, my Magical Child decided not to let this slow me down and continued on in my imaginary car. This illustrated my ability to overcome adversity and reinforced the benefits of using my imagination.

The Old Wise Man archetype presented himself as the two old women at the campfire, and the magical wisdom they bestowed upon me was that in the midst of my dilemma, I still possessed the ability to help others.

Although I wouldn't be able to see it until years later, this dream was precognitive as well. The endeavor that I was undertaking was opening a business that would offer classes in the arts, yoga, and self-exploration. There would be plenty of obstacles along the way; however, I would find imaginative ways around them. It was an undertaking that would require a great deal of hard work and nurturing. Ultimately, I had to close the business, but my efforts to make it work led me to realize that one of my greatest joys is helping others.

Many Benefits

As you can see, once you begin to work with your dreams it does not take long to discover that they rarely mean just one thing. They can offer detailed insights into future events. Remember that dreams are almost never literal, even when they are premonitory. Had I known that my grain field dream was precognitive and tried to interpret it literally, I would not have gleaned much, if any, useful information from the dream.

Precognitive dreams can offer us insights and warnings about society as well as personal lives. In her book, *The Third Reich of Dreams*, Charlotte Beradt shares a collection of dreams of hundreds of Germans that she compiled and smuggled out of Germany during the 1930s. The dreams, riddled with foreboding imagery, foretell with stunning clarity the nightmarish times that lay ahead.

After the terrorist attacks of September 11, 2001 many people realized that they had experienced prophetic dreams just prior to the tragedy. I recall a dream I had one week prior to the attacks in which evil men trapped hundreds of people on a ship and put them into tanks where they were to be attacked by sharks. The faces of the innocent people, especially the children, haunted me for hours after waking, as did the twisted faces of the men who cackled with delight as they pulled the mechanism that would release the sharks. I remember being baffled by this dream until, one week later, its tragic meaning was revealed.

Keeping a dream journal is an excellent way to work with your dreams. I recall more details about my dreams as I write them down. I also find it useful to go back and re-read certain dreams, particularly recurring dreams. Recurring dreams are often an indication of something unresolved or unacknowledged in your life or your subconscious, and their themes will continue to present themselves to you in a variety of ways until the issue is resolved.

For many years I had a recurring dream in which I was exploring an expansive Victorian mansion. Parts of the house were beautiful, and other areas were dark and mysterious, but the house as a whole was elaborate and majestic. Carl Jung felt that a house represented an image of the psyche. As I found the courage to explore and acknowledge the dark and mysterious parts of myself, I had the house dreams less frequently, until they stopped all together. As I went through my dream journals and re-read the Victorian mansion dreams, I saw how each dream had the same overarching message, but with different details pertaining to circumstances specific to the time I had the dream.

Dream journaling requires persistence and self-discipline. Although there are lots of fancy dream journals available on the market, I prefer a simple composition notebook for recording my dreams. I like the hard, sturdy covers and wide line spacing these notebooks provide.

I often have fun decorating the covers of my dream journals with stickers or doodles. My favorite composition notebook came with a Sasquatch-adorned cover. This was exciting for me because my inner Magical Child has a fascination with the idea of a hairy, nine-foot, 800-pound humanoid lurking behind the trees of North America, but I digress…

Upon waking in the morning, I record everything I can remember, starting with the way I felt just after waking from the dream. The emotions that our dreams evoke provide valuable insights into the messages they are trying to convey. I often start my dream journal entries with several adjectives describing how I felt about the dream. I also find it helpful to draw pictures of certain dream images, especially ones that are difficult to put into words. If a picture is too difficult to draw, I search on the Internet to find a similar image. I am often surprised to learn that an image that I thought to be merely a symbol in my dream is something that exists in the real world.

I once had a dream that I was looking at a beautiful constellation of stars in the night sky. As I looked up in wonder, my dream self whispered with excitement, "It's the Pleiades!" At the time, I knew only a few constellations, and when I woke the next morning I looked up the Pleiades and was amazed when pictures of the constellation exactly matched my dream image. Recognizing that the dream held multiple meanings, I looked for clues by reading the Greek myth of the Pleiades, also known as the Seven Sisters.

While I was researching, I shared the information with a close circle of my female friends, and in the process found that each of them, in their own way, also felt a strong connection to the Greek myth. Curious about this, I was guided by my inner voice to plug in each or our addresses into the GPS on my computer; I was amazed to learn that the position of each of our addresses in relation to one another created a formation on the map similar to that of the star cluster.

Naturally, we all found this exciting and began meeting regularly to explore the myth and discuss the archetypal messages it held for us. My time spent meeting with this group of close friends is one of my most cherished examples of living the Intuitive Life. It was the result of being open to my dream messages, listening to my inner voice, trusting enough to share my experience, and being open to exploring archetypal patterns.

Many people find it difficult to recall their dreams, and if this is the case for you, try the following:

1. *Set the intention: Say (out loud) to yourself, "When I wake up I will remember my dream." When said out loud and with authority, your subconscious hears your intention and seeks to comply.*

2. *Try to wake up in the middle of the night. Dreams are more easily remembered if we wake either right after or during them. I have a friend who drinks a large glass of water right before bed to ensure that she wakes up during the night to record her dreams.*

3. *Keep your dream journal next to your bed; when you wake during the night jot down key elements of the dream that will help you with later recall.*

> 4. *Do not move around a lot upon waking. Dreams evaporate quickly when we begin to move our bodies and shift into wakefulness. Lie still as you begin to wake and allow your dream to emerge and take root in your conscious mind. Give this process several minutes. I have lost important dream details by not giving them long enough to take root in my conscious mind.*

Dreamwork should be fun, so remember not to get frustrated or take yourself too seriously. Applying your sense of humor to dream interpretation will help you understand the playful logic of the subconscious mind. The subconscious loves to use puns and one-liners in dreams, so watch for them as you record your dreams. Perhaps you have a dream in which you reach into your pocket for change and come up empty-handed. You make the statement: "I have no cents." Change "cents" to "sense" and it may become clear that your subconscious is trying to make a point about your judgment in a current situation.

Conversely, you might have a dream in which everywhere you go, you are given handfuls of coins. Your subconscious may be saying that "lots of change" is coming your way.

Another important thing to keep in mind while examining your dreams is that the characters in your dreams represent various aspects of yourself. So, if you find yourself suddenly dreaming of an old classmate from elementary school, examine the personality traits of your childhood friend and decide what he or she symbolizes to you, or what archetype they represent. An exception to this is when dreaming of a loved one who has passed. Dreams are a common way in which loved ones visit us. Not every dream of a deceased loved one is a visitation, however. Visitation dreams have certain characteristics. They are usually quite vivid and involve a clear communication from your loved one, who will often appear vibrant and healthy. The dream will not be complicated and drawn out, but rather brief and to the point. Your loved one has not taken the time to reach out to you through time and space to confuse you.

Shortly after Aunt Annette died, I had a dream in which she was working happily in a garden. The sun shone so brightly on her hair that it glowed, and as she looked up from her work she smiled and blew me a kiss. The dream was short, sweet, to the point and vivid. I knew it was Aunt Annette saying goodbye and showing me that she was happily continuing her work on a higher plane.

Sometimes we become aware that we are dreaming; this is called lucid dreaming. I have the most fun in lucid dreams because I have the ability to do anything. Flying is a favorite activity of mine in lucid dreams; however, I often choose superhuman strength and agility to help me out of difficult situations. In my waking life, my lack of coordination and rhythm make me a terrible dancer but in lucid dreams my dancing is effortless and graceful. I am happy to say that I have found myself shamelessly showing off my dancing talents in many lucid dreams!

You can train yourself to lucid dream by recognizing the clues or signs that you are dreaming. For me this often occurs when I find myself in an extremely absurd situation, or suddenly transported from one location to another within the dream landscape. To encourage lucid dreaming, set your intention before going to sleep. People have varying degrees of success. You should examine your dream journal to look for recurring situations in your dreams that can tip you off that you are dreaming. Sometimes the excitement of realizing that you are dreaming can wake you up. If you realize that you are dreaming, stay calm, stay in the dream, and have fun! Remember—you can do anything you want to in a dream!

Otherworldly encounters are also possible in the dreamscape. Because dreamtime is the realm of the spirit world, you can encounter many different types of beings there, as I frequently did when we lived in the holler in West Virginia.

Occasionally, I will have friends ask me to dream for them when they are seeking insights into difficult life situations. Sometimes I know their questions and sometimes not. Either way, I will have them write their question down and give it to me in an envelope. I place the envelope under my pillow before bed and ask my guides, and the guides of my friend, to provide me with a dream that will answer their question. Interpreting these kinds of dreams can be difficult because the symbols can mean different things to me than they do to my friends. I have found that when dreaming for friends, my dreams tend to contain more literal images than when dreaming for myself.

I once had a dream for a friend in which I found myself standing in front of a red apartment door with the numbers 627 on it. Upon waking, I assumed there would be symbolic meaning to the color red and the number 627. As I described the dream to my friend, she informed me that I had seen an apartment complex where she lived decades ago. Her apartment number was 627. We looked at the circumstances surrounding her life at the time, which, to her surprise, paralleled the situation she had asked me to dream about. When I asked her what she had done then, she simply nodded her head and said, "I know, I have to do the same thing now."

Dreaming with purpose is a great way to gain valuable insights into challenging situations. I frequently ask my guides to provide dream messages that will help me navigate specific circumstances. Sometimes my guides provide a dream in which I am an observer instead of a participant; these dreams are like watching a movie and always involve a large, complex cast of characters. Other times my guides will visit me in my dream and present me with a message or an object. Sometimes the objects are literal, and often they are symbolic; sometimes they are both. I once had a dream in which a spirit guide presented me with a beautiful, oval-shaped lapis stone. Since I wasn't familiar with lapis, I considered the gift to be symbolic. Two weeks later, while visiting the Serpent Mound in Peebles, Ohio I found the exact stone in their gift shop. The information provided with the stone indicated that lapis was known for stimulating psychic abilities, something I had been working on developing at the time of my dream. I believe that my guide presented me with the energetic qualities of the stone in the dream, allowing the stone to manifest physically in my waking life.

Guides are always present and working with us, but one of the best ways to meet and work with them is in the dream world. Guides will often visit us in dreams during difficult times in which we require careful guidance; however, we can request meetings with them by asking them to meet us in our dreamscape prior to going to sleep.

In his book, *The Four Agreements: A Practical Guide to Personal Freedom (A Toltec Wisdom Book)*, Don Miguel Ruiz states: "What you are seeing and hearing right now is nothing but a dream. You are dreaming right now in this moment. You are dreaming with the brain awake. Dreaming is the main function of the mind, and the mind dreams 24 hours a day. It dreams when the brain is awake, and it also dreams when the brain is asleep. The difference is that when the brain is awake, there is a material frame that makes us perceive things in a linear way. When we go to sleep we do not have the frame, and the dream has the tendency to change constantly."

What Ruiz is saying is that wakefulness is a different form of consciousness than the dream state; wakefulness isn't more "real" than dreaming—it's just different. Examining the symbols and synchronicities that arise during wakeful consciousness, as well as our interactions with them, can bring meaning, depth, and richness to our lives.

I have applied this wisdom to my waking life for many years now and have found the results to be life-changing. As I move through each day, I am always aware of the messages and dream symbols that are coming my way, like the eagle circling above my car on two separate occasions.

Another way in which messages are provided to us in our waking dreams is through *synchronicity*, or meaningful coincidences. I find it helpful to keep track of synchronicities in my Extraordinary Awareness journal.

The wonderful thing about perceiving our waking life as a dream is that we can interpret the dream while we are experiencing it. I find this practice especially helpful when I find myself in the midst of an exceptionally weird day. You know the type, the kind of day that is so riddled with unusual events that you stop in your tracks to say, to quote

Bill Murray's character from *Scrooged*, "I am having the *weirdest* day!"

    Remembering that, as Poe said, "All that we see or seem is but a dream within a dream," helps me to see the humor in my weird days and enjoy them for what they are, a delivery mechanism for intuitive messages provided to me through Extraordinary Awareness.

    Whether waking or sleeping, dreams are an important source of intuitive guidance and wisdom, and working with them should be fun and enjoyable. Take your time when examining your dreams but remember to take a playful and lighthearted approach. When I forget to take a playful approach to my dreamwork, I often overlook funny puns and messages that provide opportunities for me to take myself less seriously.

9

SIGNS, SYNCHRONICITIES AND WORKING WITH YOUR GUIDES

Synchronistic events provide an immediate religious experience as a direct encounter with the compensatory patterning of events in nature as a whole, both inwardly and outwardly. **Carl Jung**

There are more things in heaven and earth, Horatio, than are dreamt of in your philosophy. **Hamlet**

The Intuitive Life is a life filled with messages, guides, and signposts. The purpose of cultivating the art of Extraordinary Awareness is to train us to recognize these gifts.

Once we allow our Magical Child to express and lead us into imaginative wonder, shifting into Extraordinary Awareness unfolds.

We not only become open to experiences that offer guidance, we find ourselves actively seeking them out.

When we apply the same interpretive examination to events in our daily lives that we do to our dreams, patterns and messages emerge that we would probably not otherwise notice. Coincidences become synchronicities and "happy accidents" may very well be assistance from our guides.

Recognizing guidance offered through synchronicity and developing relationships with your guides are fundamental components of the Intuitive Life. Remember the realm inhabited by symbols, archetypes, and mystical beings that I mentioned earlier? Signs, synchronicities, and guides are your ambassadors to this realm.

After I had the dream about looking up at the Pleiades, I encountered information about the star cluster and the Greek myth of the Seven Sisters everywhere. The topic of Pleiadians (a group of enlightened beings identified by Barbara Marciniak in her book *Bringers of the Dawn*) would "randomly" pop up in conversations. "Out of the blue" someone would ask me about the Greek myth of the Seven Sisters, or ask me if I'd noticed the star cluster on the horizon that night. I knew that there was nothing "random" or "out of the blue" about these synchronicities and paid close attention when they arose. I had fun reading and learning what I could about the Greek myth and found similarities to them in the events and relationships in my life. This led me to coordinate the meaningful discussion group with my close circle of friends, and to this day my ears perk up when someone mentions the Pleiades. I have yet to meet someone who feels a connection to the Pleiades that I don't have a lot in common with. In fact, it has gotten to the point that when I meet someone who mentions the Pleiades, I see it as a signpost, identifying the person as someone with whom I share a common bond.

Paying attention to the ongoing synchronicities surrounding the Pleiades has strengthened my existing relationships as well as forged new ones. In addition, the messages I received from my study gave me valuable insights to my own path and purpose in life. My examinations of the Greek myth of the Seven Sisters allowed me entrance into a world of mythical beings who soon visited me in dreams and waking life. They offered to lead me into magical realms, and I was more than willing to follow.

Signs and Synchronicities

You have a dream about an old friend you haven't seen in decades. The following day you receive a friend request on social media from this person who informs you that you have been on their mind recently, so they decided to reach out.

Someone at work suggests that you try a little-known supplement; later that day, you find a coupon on your car for that same supplement. As you walk into the store, you overhear a conversation between two people about that supplement.

You're reading a book and the author mentions an obscure event from history that you were unaware of; later that evening, you're watching a television show in which that very event is covered. The following day at the bookstore, a book about the event is prominently displayed in the store.

You wake up in the morning with a song you haven't heard in years in your head. As you're eating breakfast, a car drives by with that very song blasting through its speakers. As you're driving to work, the song comes on the radio.

Experiences like these are so common that we often dismiss them without a second thought because calculating the probabilities of these "coincidences" would probably make our heads spin.

Causality is the proposition that everything in the universe has a cause and is thus an effect of that cause. According to the Axiom of Causality, the magnitude of an effect is proportional to the magnitude of its cause, and to every action there is an equal and opposed reaction. When seemingly random events occur without a discernable cause, they are often labeled coincidence, a term that, in my opinion, provides us with a convenient excuse to dismiss offhand things we do not understand.

Carl Jung believed that coincidences that occur without causality held meaning. He coined the term "synchronicity" to describe theses meaningful coincidences. In his book *Synchronicity: An Acausal Connecting Principle*, Jung wrote:

> ...*it is impossible, with our present resources, to explain ESP, or the fact of meaningful coincidence, as a phenomenon of energy. This makes an end of the causal explanation as well, for 'effect' cannot be understood as anything except a phenomenon of energy. Therefore, it cannot be a question of cause and effect, but of a falling together in time, a kind of simultaneity. Because of this quality of simultaneity, I have picked on the term 'synchronicity' to designate a hypothetical factor equal in rank to causality as a principle of explanation.*

Jung's proposal of a non-causal explanation implied that the past does not cause the future, and opened possibilities beyond time, an approach that allowed for multidimensionality, and a timeless dimension of nature. As Einstein pointed out, *time is relative*. Jung's devotion to synchronicity led him to a deeper understanding about the psyche, the cosmos and the connectivity between the two.

Jung believed that the psyche contains the future and the present moment simultaneously. He understood instances of precognition to be of great relevance, and recorded several instances of precognitive dreams in his career.

Some physicists now hold that synchronicity is the possible result of quantum entanglement. In a 2009 paper published in the *Journal of Cosmology* titled "Synchronicity, Quantum Information and the Psyche," Francois Martin, PhD, Federico Carminati, PhD, and Giuliana Galli Carminati, PhD, wrote:

> *We suppose that the mental systems first proposed by Freud, i.e. the unconscious, pre-consciousness, consciousness, are made up of mental qu-bits. They are sets of mental qu-bits.*

The paper also describes how the conscious mind may also be entangled with matter, thus explaining coincidences in which thoughts manifest in the physical world:

> *One can possibly see synchronistic events between the mental and the material domains as a consequence of a quantum entanglement between mind and matter. For us mental and material domains of reality will be considered as aspects, or manifestations, of one underlying reality in which mind and matter are unseparated.*

The authors concluded that quantum mechanics can explain synchronistic phenomena thanks to entangled states and the collapse of the wave-function (a phenomenon in quantum mechanics in which the act of observing electrons changes their behavior).

Quantum mechanics does not, however, provide a full explanation of the phenomenon. If this were the case, every thought, dream, or event would be a synchronicity. Therefore, in my opinion, the meaning of the synchronistic event arises from the very fact that it has occurred and has been observed, making it a signpost or confirmation for an individual.

The song in your head, for example, may provide a message for you in the lyrics. The friend from your past might represent an archetypal pattern you are meant to confront or explore. The obscure event from the past may provide insights into your present and the supplement suggested by your friend may provide you with needed metabolic support.

I believe that synchronicities are valuable opportunities for learning and can provide us with important insights into our emotional and spiritual growth. They can also be a great deal of fun. When synchronicities arise, pay attention to their details and explore them. Be sure to record your synchronicities in your Extraordinary Awareness journal so that you can track and research them. They are an expression of the waking dream state, and should be explored in the same way as ordinary dreams.

Carl Jung shared an experience he had with one of his patients who had recited to him a dream in which she was given a costly piece of jewelry fashioned in the shape of a golden scarab beetle. As she was relating the dream, there was a tapping at the window. Jung opened the window and in flew a gold-green scarbaeid beetle, resembling the golden scarab in the woman's dream. Jung caught the beetle in his hand and handed it to his patient and said, "Here is your scarab."

Because this patient had been so caught in her head prior to this event, the analysis had been going nowhere, and Jung had made the decision that there was nothing further he could do. He later wrote, "I had to confine myself to the hope that something unexpected and irrational would turn up, something that would burst the intellectual retort in which she had sealed herself."

The synchronistic moment shook Jung's patient into the realization that her dream held both literal and symbolic meaning, and from that point on, Jung commented, "The treatment could now be continued with satisfactory results."

The more you pay attention to synchronicities, the more frequently they occur. This confirms that you are on the right track with your explorations.

Guides

Guides love to speak to us through synchronicity, so look for messages and signs from your guides within each synchronistic event.

So who exactly are guides? Spirit guides are beings whose purpose is to provide us with assistance and guidance throughout our lives. Guides are responsible for helping us fulfill our soul contracts, or the agreements that we make with our higher selves before we are born. Guides come in many forms, and each one serves a specific function related to helping us complete our personal soul contract. We each have guides who are with us for the duration of our lives, as well as guides who are just with us for certain periods of development. Once their job is finished they move on.

Guides are beings that exist in the non-physical realm and so do not have to "look" any particular way. They often present themselves in the form of an archetype or symbol that holds meaning for you. They can be spirits who have had physical incarnations, and sometimes can be loved ones who have passed. They can also be conscious beings that have never taken a physical form.

The first time I met one of my guides was during a guided meditation for that purpose. In the meditation, I was standing in a field and had invited my guides to introduce themselves. Before I knew it a Native American brave with a single eagle feather in his hair walked up to me and told me his name: *Little Feather*. The cliché was not lost on me, and I snapped out of my meditative state, dismissing the encounter outright.

"Right…" I scoffed, "Everyone has a Native American guide! I'm not even Native American! Why in the world would I have a Native American guide?" Once again, I chose to dismiss my experience as imaginative fancy and forget it. Later that week, Little Feather made an appearance in one of my dreams and offered me a feather. For weeks after that I would find feathers similar to the one given to me in the dream everywhere I went. I stopped questioning the existence of Little Feather and paid closer attention whenever I dreamt of him or found a feather.

I have since met several of my guides, who have presented themselves in a variety of ways. Some have introduced themselves through dreams or guided meditations, while others have shown up during Reiki sessions. A few of them appeared unexpectedly, right before my eyes, and introduced themselves and explained what guidance they were there to provide.

This is a distinction that I have noticed between my guides and other spirit entities that have presented themselves to me. My guides have always offered a name and stated their purpose. For example, one afternoon as I was driving, a rather tall man suddenly appeared in the passenger seat of my car. He was quite an imposing figure and was dressed in tribal attire that appeared to be African. By this time, I had become so accustomed to guides just showing up that his appearance didn't frighten me; in fact, I was pretty excited about it, and said, "Well hello! Who are you?"

The African shaman told me his name. He seemed to know what I was about to ask next and added. "I help with self-discipline." "Well," I chuckled, "I appreciate how difficult your job must be! Thank you for putting up with me!" My shaman guide did not find my reply as funny as I did and shot me a look that was all business before gradually fading out of sight. Although I could no longer see him, I still had the strong sense of his presence next to me as I drove along.

Guides can present themselves to you in a variety of ways—in dreams, synchronicities, or the passenger seat of your car—but when they do it will always be to offer support and guidance to you. Experiences and interactions with guides are as individual as each person having them, so be open to all possibilities.

When you are ready to meet your guides, set the intention prior to going to sleep that you will meet one or more of them in the dream realm. Or, you can use the guided meditation exercise that follows.

First, instruct that you will meet only your guide or guides. No other spirit entities may present themselves to you during this meditation. Connect with your breath, using the breath meditation in Chapter Seven. Visualize yourself being surrounded by white, protective light.

Meditation for Meeting Your Spirit Guide

Find a comfortable seated position, close your eyes, and bring your awareness to your breath. Breathe in and out through your nose and allow full deep breaths to enter. Allow your abdomen to relax and expand as the breath moves in and allow the breath to move out slowly.

Imagine that you are going down a staircase. With each breath, you count down (from 10 to 1), and go down a step, until you reach the bottom of the staircase.

At the bottom of the staircase is a doorway. You slowly open the door and step through. On the other side of the doorway you find a warm, sunny day, and a beautiful tropical beach. You walk in the sand and notice it is warm on your feet. You feel the wind against your face, smell the salt air and hear, the seagulls flying above.

As you walk along the beach, you notice a figure, or figures, off in the distance, walking toward you. As you approach one another, details about this being (or beings) come into focus (there may be more than one).

Finally, you are standing in front of each other. You see your guide clearly, and ask for their name. You can ask any questions you like and you will receive an answer. After a while, your guide presents a gift to you. This gift has a special meaning for your path and purpose. Study it carefully, then thank your guide.

When you are ready, say goodbye, and walk back along the beach in the direction of the doorway. Once you reach the doorway, climb the staircase in the same manner that you descended, taking a breath with each step and counting from 1 to 10, until you reach the top.

When you're ready, bring your awareness back into the room and slowly open your eyes. Take time to write

> in your Extraordinary Awareness journal about your meeting.
>
> Remember that you can call on your guide whenever needed for assistance and guidance.

If you don't meet a guide the first few times you set a dream intention or practice the meditation, be patient. Connecting with higher realms can take time and practice.

Balancing your energetic body and practicing meditation will help with this. Also, trust that your guides will present themselves to you only when the time is right. The more you meditate and set the intention, the easier it will be to make the connection.

Whether you have or have not connected with your guides, they are always offering their support and will leave messages for you in the form of signs and synchronicities. Pennies are a favorite item for guides, so if you start finding pennies, note your surroundings and what is on your mind. Sometimes pennies provide confirmation.

Guides also use playing cards. I once received messages and confirmations for several weeks in the form of playing cards. I kept finding the eight of hearts everywhere, on the street or sidewalk, in a used book I just purchased, and even in the pocket of a pair of jeans.

Modern playing cards evolved from Tarot, so I looked up the eight of cups (the Tarot's counterpart to the eight of hearts), which revealed a message about leaving the comfort of the familiar in pursuit of a higher, spiritual path. At the time, I was finding the cards, I was on the cusp of such a transition.

Numbers are another way you might receive messages. The 11:11 synchronicity is a common example of this. This is a phenomenon in which 11:11 is seen more frequently than can be explained by chance and for this reason 11:11 is considered to be an auspicious sign. You may notice that you glance at the clock every day at that time. St. Augustine of Hippo wrote, "Numbers are the Universal language offered by the deity to humans as confirmation of the truth." Numerology is the study of the meaning of numbers, and an exploration of numerology can provide you with insights into the messages contained in repeated numbers.

Another example is waking up at a certain time every night. Once I was researching the numerological significance of the number 44 because I had awakened several nights in a row at exactly 44 minutes past the hour, every hour. An Internet search produced several articles about the number. The first one I clicked on explained how 44 and 444 are connected to angel energy. Later that day I saw that a friend of mine had posted a picture on social media of the Archangel Michael with the number 444 prominently displayed across the photo. I took the synchronicity to be a message that some research and reading about this angel of protection was in order.

Irony is a favorite for some of my guides, so whenever I find irony in a situation, I carefully look for the lessons. Ironies are never lost on me, and I always get a chuckle when they arise, because they remind me that many of my guides have a playful sense of humor.

Often guides place thoughts or ideas straight into our heads. When something important comes to me "out of the blue," I always assume it is from my guides. So, when a thought or knowing just comes to you, trust it; it is very likely assistance from your guides. Guides will often direct you to people who are meant to be in your life. The way I met Joey is an example of this, and one of my closest friends, Michelle, was directed to me through her guides.

I had met Michelle at a writer's group that I had organized and liked her from the moment we shook hands. It was a gut feeling that was so strong I didn't question it. As Michelle shared her short story with the group, her wit, sense of playful sarcasm and writing talent were so obvious, I knew my initial gut feeling was correct. One afternoon after having only seen Michelle at a few subsequent writers' gatherings, I received a phone call from her:

"I have something for you and I was wondering if we could meet; there is something I want to tell you, but I have to do it in person." Michelle sounded nervous, and for the life of me, I couldn't guess what she might have for me. I was excited about the mystery and we agreed to meet a few days later.

The day we met, it was clear that there was something Michelle really needed to get off her mind. "Okay, here goes," she said. Then she proceeded to share with me how, during a morning meditation, one of her guides had come to her and insisted that she needed to try automatic writing. Michelle had tried automatic writing before, so this instruction didn't seem unusual, but what she was instructed to do next was. Her guide was very specific about the notebook she was to use for her automatic writing sessions, and then instructed her that she was to give me a similar notebook and tell me to do the same.

"But I hardly know her!" Michelle protested. "She'll think I'm crazy!" Her guide insisted, and once again presented her with the image of the notebook that she was to give to me.

"So, here you go." Michelle presented me with a spiral bound notebook with fairies dancing on the cover. "My guide was very specific; this is the one I'm supposed to give to you." Squinting her eyes in anticipation of what I might think, she asked, "Have you ever heard of automatic writing?"

I'm sure my enthusiastic answer surprised her. "I am very familiar with it! My grandmother used to do it; she channeled an entire autobiography that way. She tried to teach me, but I never had any luck. Tell your guide I will be happy to try, but I've never really been successful with it."

That afternoon I sat down with my new fairy-adorned notebook, centered myself with breathing exercises, said a prayer and called upon my guides before I began. The results surprised me. From the time my grandmother had introduced me to automatic writing when I was 10, until sometime in my early twenties, I had tried periodically to channel information through this method.

Automatic writing is a method used for centuries as a means to communicate with the spirit world, your subconscious, or the collective unconscious. The practice involves grounding and centering yourself, clearing the mind and entering a meditative state. You hold a pen lightly on paper, close your eyes and ask a question. If the session is successful, the pen moves on its own and the answer or a message is written on the page. My grandmother employed this method for years and wrote literally hundreds of pages, channeling everything from poetry signed by William Wordsworth to a firsthand account of his life dictated by Saint Justin the Martyr.

I had never achieved anything other than indecipherable scribble, so I was amazed at the end of my session when I learned that I had channeled a message from my grandmother. This was the beginning of an amazing journey with Michelle, each of us receiving messages from various sources over a period of two years. Some of them were predictions that came true. Some sessions produced obscure references that we never did figure out. In the end, the purpose of this journey was to bring two people together in friendship. As I got to know Michelle better, the specificity of the journals her guides insisted upon became clear. In Michelle, I had met a kindred Magical Child, and I believe the dancing fairies were meant to serve as a symbol of this.

From the beginning, Michelle and I just "got" each other, and we are freely able to play, create, and imagine in a way that we might not be as comfortable with around others. We frequently find ourselves engaged in long, imaginative conversations about such things as the nature of reality, the possibility of time travel, and the existence of parallel universes. We also play. Really play. In Michelle, I have a found an eager companion who is ready to join me in everything from cloud gazing to dragon slaying. As close as Michelle and I have become, it still fascinates me to think that we may have never become much more than friendly acquaintances had she not trusted and listened to the direction given by her guide.

Guides provide us not only with direction and assistance; they also provide us with protection. In addition to being tasked with teaching me self-discipline, my African shaman guide is also a wonderful protector, and has come to my aid on several occasions in which I found myself in the presence of threatening individuals (both living and deceased).

One of these situations occurred during a class that I was taking several years ago. There was an individual in the class who frequently bragged about his psychic abilities, particularly his ability to read other people. I often noticed him staring at other classmates and got the distinct impression that he was psychically invading their space, essentially spying on them. His behavior was an inexcusable violation of respect and privacy. It is never acceptable to try to obtain intuitive information about another person's personal life without their invitation and permission.

I noticed this guy being inappropriate in this way, so I always took extra care to surround myself with protective light in case he should ever pick me as a target. He soon did. One day while sitting in class, I noticed the intense sensation of being stared at from behind. I knew immediately who it was. I brought my attention to my protective bubble of light to buff it up. It was no use. This guy was intent on getting through. At this point I could not only feel his eyes on me, I got the clairvoyant impression of his subtle energy body standing directly behind me. He had projected his energy into my physical space!

At that moment, my African shaman appeared and in one fell swoop, grabbed the psychic assailant by the neck, pushed his psychic projection across the room and slammed him back into his physical body. "Well!" I thought. "*That's* something you don't see every day!"

For the remainder of the class my guide stood behind me with his arms folded across his chest and his eyes locked on my inappropriate classmate. I have no way of knowing what this experience felt like to my classmate, but I do know that I never caught him invading anyone's privacy after that.

I call upon my guides for protection whenever I am investigating a haunted location, practicing energy work, doing readings for others, or engaged in any situation in which I feel protection is needed. I also call upon my guides to speak through me when I find myself in situations in which carefully choosing words for the sake of the other individual is crucial.

Words hold such power that it's always important to choose them carefully. I find this practice to be doubly important during readings or when offering feedback after a Reiki session. To illustrate the power we wield with our words, imagine someone said to you something like, "You look pale, are you getting sick?" Before the suggestion you may have felt perfectly fine but now you can't stop worrying whether you're coming down with something. Before long, the stress of worrying about being sick has weakened your immune system and you end up with a cold.

My guides always do a great job of helping me find the right words so that if I end up inadvertently planting seeds in someone's mind, they're seeds of positivity. I make it a point to take my time and wait for their guidance before speaking. It doesn't always come quickly, and there have been times that pauses between words take so long that I have to explain to my client that I'm waiting for words to come through from my guides. Not only do my clients benefit from the careful selection of words, the relationship that I have with my guides benefits as trust is established and strengthened. They trust that I will wait patiently for their guidance and I place my trust in the guidance they deliver.

Relationships take time to cultivate and develop, and a relationship with your guides is no different. When you feel that you are being offered assistance from your guides, take time to acknowledge them and offer them thanks. It is also important to thank your guides when you are experiencing difficult times, as more often than not, our experiences are lessons being offered to us for the purpose of our spiritual development. When I find myself going through a challenging time, I try to remember to thank my guides for providing me with the lesson as well as the strength and patience needed to see it through. Although I have to admit thanking my guides for difficult situations isn't often my first response, I eventually get around to it in the end.

The more you notice and work with signs, synchronicities, and symbols, the more your guides will offer them to you for direction because you will have acknowledged this as a welcome form of communication.

It is important to keep in mind that, just as with the subconscious, the language of spirit is metaphor, so be sure to look at messages through the lens of metaphor, symbol and archetype, just as you do with dreamwork.

The universe is a vast and wondrous place and is filled with an amazing array of sentient beings, so it is important to keep in mind that every disembodied being who offers advice is not necessarily a spirit guide. In his lecture titled *Cultivating the Heart of Compassion*, spiritual teacher and author Ram Dass says of disembodied beings, "The thing about disembodied beings is that they're just like embodied beings, some of them are smart and some of them are not. You can't just figure that because somebody doesn't have a body, that they know anything, cuz that's off the wall! Somebody who was really caught in good and evil on this plane and then they die and they figure they'll send back a message, so they send back a message like, 'Buy canned tuna and move to Oregon' or something like that."

And so it is with these beings; as you expand your awareness to include beings that reside in other realms you may encounter them regularly. Some of these beings are your guides, and many are not. Like people, some are friendly and some are not. When encountering beings from other realms, notice the way you feel when they are present. There is a sense of peace and serenity that accompanies interactions with our guides, so notice if those sensations arise in your body. Next, ask the beings to identify and introduce themselves. Guides will do this without hesitation, while trickster beings will either outright refuse or offer riddles, sarcasm, or ridicule.

Guides work with our highest good in mind, and for the highest good for all involved. Your guides will never ask you to participate in anything that interferes with the free will or well-being of another. I have unfortunately witnessed some individuals succumb to the slippery slope of assuming that their desires or beliefs should trump the free will of others. No matter what our reasons, it is never permissible to interfere with the free will of another person, and your guides will not assist you in such behavior.

Guides will however provide you with the strength and guidance to handle situations in which the free will of another imposes difficulty or harm for you. In situations like these you can always ask for protection, but never for control over the other person's thoughts or actions. I find the Serenity Prayer offers abundant grace and peace of mind.

It is also important not to allow expectations to get in your way. Years ago, I had the privilege of participating in Lakota sweat lodge ceremonies, and each time before we began, the leader of the ceremony would remind us of the importance of being ready for anything while expecting nothing. This also applies when working with your guides. Our understanding of how these beings work is so limited that to place expectations on what our interactions with them should be is extremely limiting and short-sighted. At the same time, the more you open your mind and heart to encounters with these beings, the more extraordinary your experiences will be.

Your guides are patiently waiting for you to ask them for guidance and assistance; they seek to guide you on your path and connect you with friends and soul mates. The more you find yourself residing in Extraordinary Awareness, the more open to guidance you become. Before you know it, living intuitively becomes second nature and synchronicity will become a common occurrence that offers you insight and leads you to meaningful friendships and deeper insights about your life and the universe around you.

10

IMPLEMENTING TOOLS FOR GUIDANCE AND PROTECTION

He opened the book at random, or so he believed, but a book is like a sandy path which keeps the indent of footsteps. **Graham Greene**

It seems that these old cards were conceived deep in the guts of human experience, at the most profound level of the human psyche. It is to this level in ourselves that they will speak. **Sallie Nichols**

Years ago, I was introduced to a magical, mythical little dwarf named… well, never mind his name. The dwarf was an ass. We met at a weekend workshop for developing intuition and he came to me in the form of a deck of oracle cards. How cute and sweet I thought he was, his animated gestures and pithy expressions gracing each colorful card. His deck seemed like a fun way to seek guidance, so I purchased the cards. How wrong I was. Instead of the wit and wisdom I expected, the diminutive dude offered only sarcasm and obscurity. His answers were snarky and unclear and left me with more questions than answers. Try as I might to rephrase questions and forge a relationship with the dwarf, he continued to be oppositional and unhelpful. Eventually I tossed his deck in a drawer and forgot about him.

In addition to signs, synchronicities, and dream messages, there are tools that one can use to cultivate natural intuitive abilities. Mostly these tools are informative and helpful. Occasionally, they are nothing more than impractical novelties in the form of grouchy dwarves.

For thousands of years, cultures from all over the world have consulted such oracles as stones, pendulums, tea leaves, coins, and cards. The Greeks had the human Oracle of Delphi, the Chinese the *I Ching*, and European cultures sought guidance from the Tarot.

In the modern age, these tools are not as widely used, which is a shame because they can be a wonderful source of guidance when consulted. In addition, these tools provide a wonderful opportunity to cultivate your intuitive abilities because interpreting the messages they provide is purely intuitive work. Each tool offers a different way for you to exercise your intuition and awaken different areas of your intuitive abilities. (That is of course, as long as you're dealing with sincere tools and not the incarnation of a sassy elemental who considers himself something of a comedian.)

Some people love working with tools while others do not, and not all tools are for all people. What is wonderful about tools is that they provide yet another opportunity for you to listen to and trust your gut. If a particular tool feels right for you, explore it; if it doesn't, don't. It's that simple. Most importantly, remember to infuse your explorations with an element of childlike fun and wonder. Approach them in the same way your Magical Child approaches cloud gazing. Be sure to balance your lighthearted wonder with respect and decorum, however. Asking silly or pointless questions, or seeking guidance for something you already know the answer to is just about as unhelpful as a dwarf with an attitude.

The ability to laugh at ourselves is an important part of any kind of self- development; an experience I had recently with a friend is an excellent example of this. For several years, despite my complete absence of rhythm and coordination, I had wanted to try a Zumba class, so when a friend of mine invited me to join her for one I was excited to give it a try.

It didn't take long for us to realize that keeping up with the steps required a level of skill beyond our abilities, and I soon noticed my friend becoming frustrated. Because I had long ago embraced my inability to dance I was able to find the humor in what my attempt to follow the steps must have looked like. Occasionally, I found the image of myself so hilarious I had to stop moving altogether to laugh out loud.

At the end of the class my friend shared that she hadn't really enjoyed it, and might not come back. I urged her to give it another try and to just have fun with it. "As long as we're moving," I pointed out, "we're still getting a good workout." She agreed and not only do we both have a great laugh each time we go to class, we've learned the moves and have made considerable improvement. Our ability to laugh at ourselves provided us with the space necessary to learn from our mistakes and have fun in the process.

Apply the same approach to working with tools. Approach them with sincerity, but don't take yourself too seriously. Developing your intuitive abilities, as with any other kind of self-development, should always contain an element of fun and playfulness.

Tools for Guidance

Books

Books are probably the easiest and most accessible tools that one can use to cultivate intuition. Almost everyone has books in their home, and if you're like me you have shelves full of them. When I first began consulting books for guidance I would always choose my Bible; however, over the years I have found that any book that you are drawn to works just fine.

To use a book as a tool for guidance, begin by either standing in front of a bookshelf or by selecting several books and placing them in front you. Quiet your mind by bringing your awareness to your breath. After you have taken a few deep breaths, allow your intuition to direct you to a book. Always go with your first impulse—don't take time to think about it. When you have selected your book, call to mind your question or the issue that you are seeking guidance for. Be as specific as possible. General questions will produce general answers. If you tend to be a visual person you can close your eyes and visualize the person or situation you are inquiring about. If you are a more auditory person, carefully consider the wording of your question and then say it out loud.

Once you have clearly presented your question, open the book to any page and read wherever your eyes fall. Don't second-guess. The answer or guidance you seek will be in the text. To give an example of how this process might work, perhaps you are wondering about when something you are expecting to happen might come to pass. You select your book and open to a page in which there is a conversation between two people concerning a process that will take six months. From that you would conclude that the answer to your question is about six months.

Although this process takes very little time, it is important not to rush through it. If you feel uncertain about the message, close the book, ask for clarification and try again by opening to another page. Generally, you do not want to seek clarification for the same question more than twice because it leads to doubt and confusion. If you feel you are not receiving clear information, try clearing your mind and wording your question in a different way.

Selecting a book and a page is a wonderful way to explore what your initial gut sensations feel like because there is nothing at stake. There is no need to worry or question your initial impulse—just go with it. Be sure to make a mental note of what your initial impulse feels like so that you'll recognize it in the future.

Pendulums

A pendulum is a small weighted object connected to a piece of thread or chain. Many pendulums consist of quartz crystal suspended on a chain, although almost anything can be used as a weight and fashioned into a pendulum. I remember several instances of my grandmother tying the wedding ring of an expecting woman to a string and holding it over her belly to learn the sex of the baby. If the ring began to swing in a circular fashion a girl could be expected. If the swinging was in a back and forth direction a boy was on the way.

In his book *Mysteries*, Colin Wilson shares some amazing accounts of the way in which archaeologist Thomas Lethbridge experimented with pendulums to locate buried objects with great success. Throughout history dowsing has been known for its ability to locate water, gold, oil, and other minerals. In France, physicians once used the pendulum in making diagnoses.

Pendulums can be found on the Internet and in New Age shops. Choosing the right one for you is a simple exercise in trusting your intuition. To select a pendulum, hold various ones in your hand to get a sense of the one that feels right for you. Again, trust your first impulse and don't second-guess.

To use your pendulum, sit or stand comfortably. Extend the palm of your left hand upward. Hold the upper end of the chain between your thumb and forefinger and dangle the pendulum a few inches above your palm. Ask to be shown what a "yes" answer will look like and wait for the pendulum to swing. For me "yes" answers are almost always represented by a circular swing. Once you have established what direction a yes swing will be, stop the pendulum and ask it to show you the "no" direction. For me this is almost always a back and forth motion. The motions can be different for everyone.

Once you have established what your answers will look like, bring your awareness to your breath. Take a few deep breaths and focus intently on your question. Be careful with your questions because it is possible to override the movements of the pendulum with your will. If you have a great deal of emotional involvement in the outcome, it is better to ask someone who has no interest in the outcome to use the pendulum for you.

Limit your inquiries to simple yes or no questions and keep them to one topic at a time. It is better to ask a series of simple questions, rather than asking one complicated question. You will receive clearer answers.

Just as with books, approach your work with the pendulum with a sense of wonder and fun and avoid consulting it too frequently or for matters that are easily puzzled out on your own.

Oracle Cards

Oracle cards are card decks, usually decorated with colorful and symbolic artwork, used for divination and spiritual guidance. Most large bookstores carry oracle cards galore. There are as many types of oracle decks as there are personalities—Angel Cards, Animal Totem Cards, Vision Quest Cards, and Archetype Cards. I even have a deck of Baseball Tarot cards.

The ways in which you can use the cards are as varied as the cards themselves. Some decks, like the Grace Cards by Cheryl Richardson, are as simple to use as closing your eyes, asking a question and choosing a card. Other decks, like *The Way of Cartouche* oracle by Murry Hope, provide detailed information for the seeker through complicated spreads.

The story about how *The Way of Cartouche* cards came to me is pretty amazing. One year after Joey's Aunt Annette had passed away, some friends of ours who owned a bookstore in New Jersey contacted us. The night before, a donated bag of books had been left at the back door of their shop. As they were going through the contents, they were especially intrigued by the *Cartouche* cards that they found in the bag, so they opened the box to look at the book inside. On the inside cover of the book Aunt Annette had written her first and maiden name, which our friends immediately recognized because Aunt Annette had been a regular customer of theirs. As a matter of fact, she introduced us to the book store owners, who have been close friends and creative collaborators of ours for nearly 20 years now.

Knowing that we would want the deck, our friends immediately put it in the mail to us. In the meantime, we contacted our Uncle Robert to see if he recalled the deck, but he did not. Since the book contained Aunt Annette's maiden name and she had been married to Robert for over 20 years before she had passed, we deduced that the cards had not been in her possession for at least that long, perhaps longer. That the cards had made their way to our friends' bookstore after 20-plus years, and near the one-year anniversary of her death astounded us. We felt sure that it was Aunt Annette's way of offering us a unique gift from the other side.

When selecting an oracle deck, take your time and listen to your inner voice (or, like our *Cartouche Cards*, they might find their way to you!). Choose something that speaks to you or that makes a statement about who you are. Although many of these decks come with books that outline a variety of complicated spreads that can be used, don't worry about that in the beginning. Simply sit quietly with your deck in hand, bring your awareness to your breath and focus your mind on your question. You can select one card or several. You can either select the cards randomly without looking at them, or spread them out face up and select the ones that call out to you. Look at the pictures and let them narrate a story to you. Allow a message to emerge from the story.

Consulting oracle cards is a wonderful way to gain more insight into situations and can be a lot of fun. Relax and have fun. Like working with books, you can always inquire a second time for more clarification if something is unclear, but avoid asking the same question over and over.

I Ching

The *I Ching*, or Book of Changes, is one of the oldest books in the world, and its wisdom has been consulted for thousands of years. Carl Jung consulted the *I Ching* throughout his life and was quite impressed by its clear answers to his questions. In his foreword for Richard Wilhelm's translation of the *I Ching*, Jung wrote:

> *The I Ching does not offer itself with proofs and results; it does not vaunt itself, nor is it easy to approach. Like a part of nature, it waits until it is discovered. It offers neither facts nor power, but for lovers of self-knowledge, of wisdom—if there be such—it seems to be the right book. To one person its spirit appears as clear as day; to another, shadowy as twilight; to a third, dark as night. He who is not pleased by it does not have to use it, and he who is against it is not obliged to find it true. Let it go forth into the world for the benefit of those who can discern its meaning.*

The *I Ching* consists of 64 hexagrams, which are figures made up of six stacked horizontal lines. Each line of the hexagram is either yang (an unbroken, solid line), or yin (a broken line). Hexagrams are formed by combining the three-lined symbols, called *trigrams*, in various combinations. Each of the three lines in a trigram can either be straight or broken. Each of the 64 hexagrams has a specific meaning that relates to the question being posed.

With so many translations of the *I Ching* on the market, finding one that is easy to use and understand can be challenging. *The Toltec I Ching*, by William Douglas Horden, contains 64 beautifully written chapters each combined with beautiful full-color interpretations by Martha Ramirez-Oropeza. *The Toltec I Ching* combines the ancient wisdom of the Toltecs and the Chinese and provides easy to understand interpretations of the hexagrams.

Rune Stones

The word *rune* comes from the Norse word Runa, which means "secret" or "mystery." It is not known exactly how old the runes are. Rune-like symbols appear in early cave drawings, and were used for thousands of years by the nomadic tribes of Europe. Runes are the letters in a set of

Germanic alphabets known as runic alphabets, which were used before the adoption of the Latin alphabet.

Rune stones for divination come in a set of 24 stones inscribed with ancient alphabetic symbols, plus a pouch and book of instructions defining the symbols.

One way to use rune stones is to sit in quiet meditation on a question while holding the pouch. After a few moments, reach into the pouch and pull out a stone. You can do a draw every morning for insights into the day ahead. For more complex questions, draw three for a Three Rune Spread.

Spirit Boards

Spirit boards, also known as talking boards, have been in use for quite some time. Early spirit boards were homemade devices in which a glass or pointing device was placed on an alphabet-adorned piece of paper.

Most people have become familiar with the talking board known as the Ouija. The Ouija was born in the late 19th century, and by the 1960s was mass produced by Parker Brothers, a game manufacturer. (Parker Brothers was later sold to Hasbro, which now holds all the Ouija rights and patents.)

My own experiences with the Ouija board began at around the age of six or seven, through my grandmother who always brought it along with her whenever she came to visit us.

My grandmother was captivated by the Ouija board, and consulted it frequently. I remember watching with amazement and wonder as my parents consulted the board with my grandmother. When I was very young, I was only permitted to watch but not to participate. I remember watching the triangular planchette move across the board with fascination as I eagerly yearned for the day that I would be allowed to use it. Finally, the day arrived. When I was 15, my grandmother came to live with us in Arizona. She gifted me her spare Ouija board, insisting that it be treated with respect and not be used as a toy or parlor game. She instructed me to say a prayer for protection and to surround myself with white light before consulting the board.

For weeks afterward, my girlfriends and I would gather in my bedroom after school and consult the board. It started out quite fun and innocent, but it wasn't long before our Ouija sessions took a turn toward the dark. One afternoon, after we had inquired if anyone was present, the planchette moved back and forth between the letters "M" and "A," spelling out the word "Mama." Once we had established that the entity referred to itself as "Mama," we received a series of dark messages and threats. Disturbed by what had come through, we decided to end the session for the day and put the board away. Worried that she might take the board away, I refrained from telling my grandmother about what had happened.

Our next several attempts with the Ouija board resulted in contact with the Mama entity, regardless of our prayers and efforts to contact more pleasant beings. With each session, the messages grew darker and more threatening, until finally out of nervous frustration we began to mock and shame the entity, calling on it to prove that it was as powerful as it claimed. Mama complied.

I began to have terrible nightmares and would awaken in the middle of the night to find that my radio had come on by itself, emitting disturbing voices from the speakers. One night I was awakened by a crackly voice coming through the radio taunting, "I'm watching you!"

Things fell off my dresser and shelves as if they had been knocked off. Once, as I was brushing my hair in the mirror of my vanity, I had a vision of my hair growing long and black as my facial features distorted to those of a haggard old woman.

The nightmares continued until I finally shared with my grandmother our encounter with Mama and the troubling things I had been experiencing ever since. She was furious with me for the reckless way in which we had engaged the Mama entity and because I had not come to her sooner. We worked together to clear the entity from the house and to surround me with protective energies, and after several weeks things returned to normal.

As a result of my carelessness, my grandmother took the Ouija board back and insisted that I refrain from ever using one again. This was an order that I was happy to comply with until years later when my grandmother passed. When I was 21, she was killed in a car accident (something she had predicted years earlier in a letter to my uncle). As our family was packing up her belongings we each took something that held special meaning for our memory of her. Because she had always mentored and encouraged my writing, I took all of her notebooks, including her Ouija board transcripts and the Ouija board that she had given me all those years before.

Eager to communicate with her, I set the board up as soon as I got home that evening. Placing my hands gently on the planchette I asked, "Grandma, are you here?" The pointer moved to spell out. "Yes." "Do you have a message for me?" The reply came quickly: "I told you never to use this."

Since our family had decided to maintain my grandmother's trailer in Show Low, Arizona after she passed, I returned the board to her home the first opportunity I got and refrained from using any talking boards for years. Approximately 20 years after I received the message from my grandmother through the Ouija board, I communicated with her through an angel talking board that a friend had brought along on one of our trips to Point Pleasant. Our group of friends managed to communicate with her for quite some time that night and she even managed to help mend a dispute between two brothers that were with us that night.

Because I had such a positive experience communicating with my grandmother that evening, I decided to ask my mother to send me my grandmother's Ouija board, thinking perhaps my experiences with it moving forward would only be positive. I soon learned that was not to be the case.

My friend Michelle had been having recurring dreams in which her mother, who had passed away several years before, was trying to communicate something to her. Since Michelle had been unable to determine what the message was, we decided to try to contact her on my grandmother's Ouija board.

Following my grandmother's advice from years before, we said a prayer and surrounded ourselves with white, protective light. We also lit a candle and some incense.

When we asked if anyone was present, the planchette moved to rest on the moon. Thinking it might be just a fluke, we joked, "Is this Moon?" The pointer moved over to rest on the clouds. After a few minutes, the planchette moved over the alphabet and spelled out "I'm looking for Zozo."

"Who is Zozo?" we inquired.

The planchette moved to spell out "Are you Zozo?" It was clear at this point that we had encountered a trickster spirit.

After we assured the entity that we were not Zozo, the pointer began to move back and forth between the Z and the O, spelling out Zozo over and over. I got a sense of the entity laughing and could hear it in my mind.

At this point we realized that we weren't going to reach Michelle's mother or engage in productive conversation with the trickster spirit. Just as we decided to end the session and pack up the board the entity, spelled out "Actually, I am Zozo."

Baffled by this experience, I decided to call my friend Rosemary Ellen Guiley who has done extensive research on Ouija boards and the experiences people have had with them. She was writing a book about these experiences when I contacted her.

Rosemary was quite familiar with the Zozo entity, and shared with me that people all over the world have encountered it during Ouija sessions. Interestingly enough, there seems to be a correlation between Zozo and the Mama entity and they are often encountered during Ouija sessions at the same time, sometimes fighting for control of the board. Encounters with Zozo are so common, in fact, that Rosemary has since co-written a book with Darren Evans titled *The Zozo Phenomenon.*

Many people find that they only have positive experiences with the Ouija, but for many more, the boards are like a beacon for lower energy forms and the bottom feeders of the spirit realm, entities like Zozo and Mama. Because of my experiences, I don't recommend using them because they are too risky; you can never be sure who or what you'll end up communicating with. If you feel absolutely compelled to use a spirit board I strongly recommend only doing so if you are able to have an experienced medium present, and then only after you have taken precautions for your energetic protection. (I feel perfectly comfortable, for example, consulting the Ouija board with Rosemary because of her extensive knowledge and experience with them.)

I have heard countless storied from folks who, thinking the board was nothing more than a game or a novelty item, ended up having frightening experiences and we resigned never to use one again.

Tools for Protection

Protecting your energetic body is just as important as protecting your physical body. While practices such as yoga, pranayama, and meditation help to strengthen and support your energetic body, there are tools that can offer additional support. I recommend incorporating some of the following into your daily routine to support and maintain your energetic body and protect yourself from external negative influences. Some of these tools will appeal to you more than others, and you will find that you will be drawn to the ones that are best suited for you. I recommend trying each of them so that you get a sense of how each influences the way you feel.

Essential Oils

Essential oils are naturally occurring, volatile (meaning they vaporize), aromatic compounds found in plants. They protect plants against environmental threats and play a role in plant pollination. Essential oils have long been used for beauty treatments and medicinal practices, as well as for food preservation and preparation.

Essential oils have the highest vibrational frequencies of any measured natural substance. Therapeutic-grade essential oils have frequencies that resonate with the electrical field of the human body (a healthy human body has a frequency ranging from 62 to 72 MHz.)

Higher frequency oils have been shown to support the emotional and energetic body, while oils with lower frequencies offer support to the physical body.

The wonderful thing about essential oils is, not only do they support you energetically, they also provide therapeutic benefits through the way that they smell—they have benefits that can be experienced through inhalation.

Essential oils are not currently regulated, so it is important to buy from certified companies who provide only pure, therapeutic-grade oils.

Some oils that provide excellent energetic support are rosemary, frankincense, sandalwood, and myrrh. Rose essential oil has the highest frequency at 320 MHz. However, rose is also the most expensive; one small bottle requires the distillation of thousands of pounds of rose petals.

Essential oils can be used aromatically by diffusing the oils into the air or applying them topically. Diffusers are specifically designed to break essential oils into small particles and disperse them into the air. Diffusing essential oils promotes feelings of peace, relaxation, satisfaction, and overall wellness. Essential oils can be applied topically to the skin in areas such as the feet, wrists, chest, or behind the ears. Because they are very concentrated, essential oils can be quite strong. It is a good idea to dilute the oil by combining it with a carrier oil such as coconut oil before applying it to the skin.

The age-old adage "you get what you pay for" applies to the purchase of essential oils. The process of growing, harvesting, distilling, and distributing essential oils is very technical and costly, so price will almost always equate to quality. If the price seems too good to be true, it probably is.

Sage

For centuries sage has been known for its ability to clear away negative energy, including fear, anger, and lower energy forms. Indigenous peoples burn dried bundles of sage to clear the energies as a traditional part of their ritual ceremonies. This process is known as "smudging." Smudge sticks are bundles of dried sage leaves and can be purchased on the Internet or in almost any metaphysical or New Age store.

New scientific research shows that sage smoke clears bacteria, including staphylococcus, out of the air; these antibacterial benefits last for quite some time after the smoke clears.

To smudge, have on hand a bowl or seashell for catching falling ash. Hold the sage bundle over the bowl/shell and light it. Then move the bundle around the person or place you wish to clear. Blow on or wave the flame with your hand to create more smoke as needed. I like to say a prayer or set an intention as I am smudging, depending on what I am clearing. Once you have finished smudging, you can gently extinguish the bundle by pressing it into the bowl or seashell, or into a bowl of damp sand.

Incense

Like sage smoke, incense smoke is believed to be cleansing and purifying, and has been part of the ritual cleansing and purification of sacred spaces for thousands of years. Frankincense, burned during Catholic Mass since the 11th century, is now known to have antiseptic and disinfectant properties.

You smudge using the smoke of incense to cleanse away any negative energies in the same way that you use sage. It is important to select incense that does not contain chemicals or artificial perfumes, as the chemical components offer no therapeutic value. I prefer Satya Sai Baba brand Nag Champa. This brand of incense, which is an aromatic blend of resins, gums, spices, flowers, and oils, was created by Indian guru and philanthropist Sathya Sai Baba.

It has long been believed that the smoke of incense carries prayers to the heavens, and it is frequently used during prayer and meditation. I also use it whenever seeking divine guidance with the various tools and oracles listed above.

Epsom Salt

The neutralizing benefits of salt have been known for centuries, and it is widely used for removing negativity. After I return home from a busy or negative place, I always take a bath or a shower using Epsom salt. In the shower I put a small amount of salt into my hands and rub it into the skin. In addition to clearing the energetic field, it is also exfoliating! You can also add the salt to a bath. If I take a bath instead of a shower, I ladd a few drops of my favorite essential oils.

I notice the neutralizing effect of the salt on my energetic body immediately. I always regret it if I don't take this extra step after visiting such places as graveyards and extremely haunted locations.

Bells and Chimes

The vibration of ringing bells breaks up negative and stagnant energy in the air. Bells and chimes leave a crystal-clear energy field in a room; the frequency of this energy will depend on the size of the bell or chime and the type of material it is made of.

Clearing a space using sound is as simple as ringing your bell or chime. You will be able to tell that the energy has improved because the note from a bell will sound much clearer and last much longer afterward.

I have used this method of clearing in my home to great affect when I have encountered hitchhiking ghostesses who have followed me home after an investigation. Usually, their reasons for tagging along are innocent curiosity. On only one occasion was I followed by something that required more measures than a ringing bell to get rid of it.

Crystals

Crystals and gemstones transmute and magnify various energies. Quartz crystal is widely used in electronic devices because of its conductivity. Quartz is the most common form of crystal on Earth, and its colors vary to include rose quartz, smoky quartz, amethyst, and citrine.

Crystals that clear negative energies include amethyst, obsidian, clear quartz, rose quartz, smokey quartz and lapis lazuli (to name a few). When choosing crystals, use your intuition. With eyes closed, hold them in your hand and "listen" to how each one affects your body.

I take my amethyst and quartz crystals along with me for protection when I do investigations. When I give readings, I make sure to have the oval lapis stone gifted to me by one of my spirit guides.

You will need to periodically cleanse your crystals from accumulated negativity by placing them in direct sunlight or moonlight for a few hours. Placing them in a bag of salt for a few hours also works well.

Visualization

The benefits of visualization have been studied for years, and studies reveal that thoughts produce the same effects on the body as actions. Mental imagery affects cognitive processes in the brain that control motor function, attention, perception, and memory. Visualization affects the energetic body as well.

Use visualization to surround yourself with protective white light. Close your eyes and take a few deep breaths to quiet your mind. Each time you inhale, imagine a beautiful, bright white light coming in through the crown of your head and surrounding your entire body. Feel the warmth of the light protecting and supporting you. After several breaths, expand the light into a protective bubble around your body. Make it as wide and as bright as you desire. After a few moments, slowly open your eyes, confident that you are surrounded by the protective energies of the light.

Prayer

Research has repeatedly shown the effectiveness of prayer. Thoughts backed by intention are a powerful form of energy, and when you practice prayer with heartfelt intention you emit these energetic signals into your surrounding environment.

A favorite of mine since childhood is *The Lord's Prayer*. I wasn't surprised to learn that author Dana Williams discovered a correspondence between the prayer's phrases and the seven major chakras in the body and the 12 archetypal paths of life.

Marianne Williams explains this connection in her book, *The Lord's Prayer, The Seven Chakras, The Twelve Life Paths: The Prayer of Christ Consciousness as a Light for the Auric Centers and a Map through the Archetypal Life Paths of Astrology*.

Although The Lord's Prayer is a wonderful way to provide grounding and protection, certainly any prayer, affirmation, or mantra that provides you with a sense of security can be used.

Breath

The practice of pranayama is used to balance the emotional, energetic, and physical bodies, and a daily practice of focused breath work is extremely beneficial. Clearing the energetic body using breath can be as easy as taking several slow, deep breaths; however, the Alternate

Nostril practice outlined in Chapter Seven is also an excellent way to clear energetic channels in the body.

Experiment with the tools in this chapter and remember to approach them in a playful and curious way. Be sure to listen to your inner voice to discern which ones feel right for you. Use your Extraordinary Awareness journal to write about your experiences as you experiment with each of these tools. Finally, remember not to become dependent on tools. Aunt Annette used to say, "You only need tools until you don't need them anymore," meaning the actual tool is just a means to bring you into certain energetic and emotional states. Once you become adept at using these tools, you can automatically create the same energetic results by calling them to mind.

11

PUTTING IT ALL TOGETHER AND LIVING THE INTUITIVE LIFE

Personal relationships are the fertile soil from which all advancement, all success, all achievement in real life grows. **Ben Stein**

If the doors of perception were cleansed everything would appear to man as it is, infinite. **William Blake**

When I was a kid I invented a game that I called "What If?" The game was simple. It consisted of posing ridiculous questions that conjured hilarious images. As a child I questioned everything, so I suppose it's no surprise that the question that started the game popped into my head one day.

"I wonder why a human's arms are not longer?" (Being short, I'm sure I was contemplating the huge advantage that having longer arms would offer).

From there my imagination took off and before I knew it, I was visualizing myself with longer and longer arms until finally the image of my knuckles dragging on the ground sent me into a giggle fit. (Giggle fits were quite common for me as a kid. I was always getting scolded for my inability to regain my composure after a particularly long giggle fit—especially at the dinner table.) From there my mind started to race. The questions wouldn't stop. My all-time favorite was, "What if everyone in the world had a rainbow clown afro?" You have to admit, picturing everyone you know with a giant, rainbow afro can keep you busy and giggling for a long, long time. Isn't imagination wonderful?

I guess I never stopped playing the "What If" game. I just started asking different kinds of questions. Questions like:

What if I decided to take myself less seriously? What type of fun and adventure would that lead to?

What if I listened to my inner voice? What kind of relationships would it lead me to?

What if I trusted my senses and believed my experiences? How might that enrich my life?

What if I paid attention to signs and synchronicities? What kind of guidance would that provide?

One common denominator surfaced with the answers to these questions, and that denominator was "meaningful connections." The Intuitive Life is the happy life because it ultimately leads us to the most valuable asset we can ever obtain—meaningful relationships.

In his 2015 TED Talk about Happiness, psychiatrist Robert Waldinger shared the results of the 75-year Harvard study on adult development, of which he is the director. The study, which began tracking the lives of 724 young men in 1938, has 60 survivors in their 90s as of this writing. The results of the study might surprise you. When people think of happiness, they often associate it with wealth. But here's the thing—People who are more *socially connected* are happier and healthier, and live longer. In addition, this study reveals that, ultimately, it is not the *number* of relationships one has, but the *quality* of those relationships.

Pursuit of quality relationships brings meaningful connections to our lives. Waldinger stated in his talk that "The people in our study who were happiest in their retirement were the people who had actively worked to replace workmates with playmates."

Playmates. I love that word! Playmates are what we find when we follow our inner Magical Child and live the Intuitive Life. Playmates are what make our lives rich and meaningful. Not just casual playmates, though—playmates that we share deep connections with, playmates who see the world the way we do, playmates who "get" us. Of all the wonderful benefits of learning to trust and follow your inner voice, making meaningful connections is the most valuable. These connections lead us to happier, healthier, and longer lives; lives enriched by the presence of the inner Magical Child of our playmates.

Another reason I like the word playmates is because of its two roots: *play* and *mate*, which makes me think of the world of theatre and storytelling, where the inner Magical Child is truly honored and encouraged. Turns out that my game of "What If" has been used by some of the most important directors and teachers as a way to help hone the imagination and intuition of the playmates: the members of a theatre company! As a matter of fact, one of Joey's first plays for young audiences was called *What If*, and it came out of the very same improvisational free play that I used when I was a child.

What this journey is about is living from the heart.

Living from the heart is important because thanks to the HeartMath Institute, we now know that the heart sends more information to the brain than the brain sends to the heart. The Magical Child knows this instinctively. I remember how, when my children were very little, I would tuck them in at night and they would recite to me the name of every person they loved. It was a long list, essentially consisting of *every person* they knew. It was as if they felt so much love in their little bodies that they verbally had to express it each night. I imagine that the love that so overwhelmed them was a love they felt not only toward the people in their lives, but also toward everything they encountered, every moment of every day.

The way to our Magical Child is through our intuitive heart. By allowing our hearts to be open and not guarded, we experience a sense of wonder and adventure. Through our intuitive heart we find our way toward imaginative play and allow ourselves to be open to experiences that fall just outside of our understanding of the natural world. It is only through our intuitive heart that we can allow ourselves to be open to the signs and synchronicities that present themselves all around us. It is through our intuitive heart that our guides speak to us and lead us to opportunities, friendships, and perhaps even love.

We live in an ego-driven world, a world in which how we live is determined by what we've been taught to believe about ourselves and about the world around us. Ego is a tool we use for navigating the material world, but perhaps not the best tool. Ego relies on a set of beliefs that will always lead to *judgment*. Judgment inevitably leads to a closed mind and closed heart. What if we lived in a world in which open minds and open hearts prevailed? Imagine the healing that could take place in a world in which the heart prevailed over the ego.

Now more than ever the world needs people willing to trust their intuitive hearts enough to remember that they are part of the fabric of a living, breathing multiverse and that the whole is greater than the sum of its parts.

The world needs the Magical Child, the child that sees the beauty in all things, trusts the power of the imagination, accepts that anything is possible and understands that things do not always have to be seen to be believed. It is a journey well worth the effort, for it brings much needed healing, peace, satisfaction, and fulfillment into the world.

The world also needs the Divine Child, the Child that enjoys a special union with the Divine, and lives immersed in divine innocence while simultaneously tapping into the guidance of the inner voice. It is my hope that the exercises and experiences shared in this book will assist you on your journey, and that as you embark on it you will infuse it with the sense of fun and wonder that only a child can bring. It is a lifelong journey that will lead you home to yourself. The more you engage in the practices outlined in the book, the closer you will come to your ultimate destination.

The world needs people who are willing to trust their experiences, whether they be a quiet whisper from the inner voice, an overwhelming gut feeling, or an encounter with a disembodied being. It needs people who are willing to cultivate a relationship with their guides and explore the language of symbols and synchronicities.

The world needs people who recognize that right now, in this moment, they are dreaming, and are willing to move through each day ready and open to the messages and dream symbols coming their way. The world needs people who are willing to open their intuitive hearts and make meaningful connections with others.

The world needs *you*.

Only by quieting our minds and tuning into our heart and body can we reconnect with the little voice within. Once we have cultivated this process, we can learn to achieve an extraordinary awareness that develops natural intuitive abilities.

The practices of grounding, yoga, meditation, and pranayama help us break our identification with the ego and trust our intuitive abilities and the workings of the intuitive heart. The HeartMath Institute studies prove what yogis and shamans have known for thousands of years—that the heart is at the center of our intuitive ability and our bodies are the instruments through which we perceive information.

Once we have mastered the art of grounding, breathing, quieting the mind, and tuning into the body simultaneously, we can expand our awareness to hear the inner voice. Because much of this information is presented to us through symbols and archetypes, living a life of Extraordinary Awareness requires thoroughly familiarizing ourselves with these languages. The practices mentioned in this book are tools to help you on your journey, but like any new practice, each takes time to develop into a habit. Take your time and be patient with yourself, maintaining that childlike sense of playfulness and wonder we all came into the world with.

Stay active with your Extraordinary Awareness journal now that you have completed the exercises in this book. As you change, the exercises will yield better and better results, and you will be able to track your progress. Go back whenever needed to look for patterns, recurring messages, and symbols. I am always pleasantly surprised, and sometimes even amazed, when I go back and read the entries in my journal. Revisiting your journals is a great way to review your spiritual evolution. Remember, never take yourself too seriously; the joy is in the journey, not the destination. The journey is a magical one, one that responds to our sense of wonder by bringing us to important crossroads at precisely the right moment.

I'd like to leave you with one final meditation, designed to open your intuitive heart and connect it with the multiverse. It is a guided meditation, and the best way to practice it is to have someone you love read it to you, or, record it and play it back as often as you like.

Heart Meditation

Lie on your back with your legs and arms extended. Let your feet roll gently outward and allow your palms to rest comfortably, facing upward. Bring your awareness to your breath and begin to take slow, deep breaths as you allow yourself to gently settle into this position.

After you have taken several rounds of deep, cleansing breaths from the diaphragm and have settled comfortably into this position, bring your awareness to heart center. In the center of your chest visualize a bright, shining light the size of an apple.

In your mind's eye see this brilliant, white light emanating from the center of your chest. Feel the warmth of that light, and with your next inhale expand the light until it becomes large enough to surround your entire body. Feel your body suspended and protected by the warmth of this brilliant, white light.

Take a deep breath and see the light expand until it becomes the size of your room. Feel the warmth of the light as it expands outward from your body to fill the room around you.

With your next inhale expand that white light further until it encompasses your entire town. Feel the warmth of the light as it expands outward from your body to surround your town. Visualize your town completely suspended in this brilliant, white light.

With your next inhale expand the light even more until it encompasses your entire state. Visualize your entire state encompassed by this protective, healing white light.

As you inhale again grow the white light even larger so that it expands to encompass your entire country. See your country gently held in this brilliant white light.

Inhaling once more, gently expand the light until it becomes the size of the world. Visualize the entire world surrounded by this brilliant, loving white light.

As you inhale again, expand that white light even larger until it reaches out to the farthest corners of the universe. There is no limit to the reach of this light; it touches everything in this and every universe with its warm, healing love. Stay in this place for a few moments as you take some deep breaths. Feel yourself connected by this white light to everything in the multiverse.

After a few moments gently draw the white in until it encompasses the planet. Feel the planet supported and surrounded by the brilliant white light as you inhale again and slowly start to bring the light in until it encompasses your country.

Feel the warmth of the light as it surrounds your country as you inhale and gently draw it in closer until it encompasses only your state.

Inhale once more to draw the light closer so that it encompasses only your town. Visualize your town bathed in this brilliant light as you begin to draw it in closer until it encompasses your house.

As you visualize your house surrounded by the warmth of the light, slowly inhale to draw it in a little further until it fills only your room.

Feel the warmth of the light filling your room as you inhale slowly and draw it closer so that it surrounds only your body.

Feel your body suspended in the warmth of this protective light as you slowly bring it back to your heart center and back to the size of an apple.

> As you feel the warmth of this radiant white light emanating from your heart center, know that this light is the energy of your intuitive heart. It is yours to share with your community, your country, your world, your universe, and the multiverse whenever you like.
>
> When you are ready, bring your awareness into your fingers and toes, wiggle them, and take a deep breath. Come on to your right side with your next exhale. Bring your right arm under your head for support and place your left hand, palm down, in front of your heart center. Take a moment here before gently pushing yourself back up into a seated position. Once seated, take a few deep breaths before making an entry about the experience in your Extraordinary Awareness journal and continuing on with your day.

I wish you love and happiness on your journey. I hope it leads you to mermaids and monkeys, to ghostesses and guides. I hope it brings you opportunities for adventure and leads you to the intersection of a crossroads at precisely the moment your Magical playmates happen to be crossing the same intersection.

And never stop asking "What If?"

About the Author

Tonya Madia is a Registered Yoga Teacher, Reiki Master Teacher and Licensed Massage Therapist. She is passionate about helping others on their journey. Her lifelong experiences with the paranormal led her to the field of paranormal investigating, and she has been working in the field since 2009. Tonya offers workshops on developing intuition, yoga, meditation, and dreamwork.

Tonya has written articles about clairvoyance, yoga, and meditation, and is the co- writer of the book for the award-winning short musical, "The Think it Thru Revue," which toured the southwest United States promoting abstinence and teen pregnancy prevention.

To learn more about her visit: www.tonyamadia.com.

Bibliography

Almeder, Robert F. *Death and Personal Survival: The Evidence for Life After Death*. Lanham, MD: Rowman and Littlefield, 1992.

Andrews, Ted. *Animal-Speak: The Spiritual & Magical Powers of Creatures Great & Small*. St. Paul, MN: Llewellyn, 2005.

Beradt, Charlotte. *The Third Reich of Dreams*. Wellingborough, England: The Aquarian Press, 1985.

Brennan, Barbara Ann. *Hands of Light*. New York: Bantam Books, 1988.

Brown, Brené. *The Power of Vulnerability*. TEDxHuston, 2010. https://www.youtube.com/watch?v=iCvmsMzlF7o

Chenglin, Liu, Wang Xiaohua, Xu Hua, Liu Fang, Dang Ruishan, Zhang Dongming, Zhang Xinyi, Xie Honglan, and Xiao Tiqiao. 2014. "X-Ray Phase-Contrast CT Imaging of the Acupoints Based on Synchrotron Radiation." *Journal of Electron Spectroscopy and Related Phenomena* 196:80–84.

Evans, Darren and Rosemary Ellen Guiley. *The Zozo Phenomenon*. New Milford, CT: Visionary Living, 2016.

Gilbert, Elizabeth. Your Elusive Creative Genius. TED2009, 2009. https://www.ted.com/talks/elizabeth_gilbert_on_genius

Hagelin, John S., Maxwell V. Rainforth, Kenneth L. C. Cavanaugh, Charles N. Alexander, Susan F. Shatkin, John L. Davies, Anne O. Hughes, Emanuel Ross, and David W. Orme-Johnson. 1999. "Effects of Group Practice of the Transcendental Meditation Program on Preventing Violent Crime in

Washington, D.C.: Results of the National Demonstration Project." *Social Indicators Research* 47 (2): 153–201.

Hameroffa, Stuart and Roger Penrose. 2014. "Consciousness in the Universe: A Review of the 'Orch OR' Theory." *Physics of Life Reviews* 11 (1): 39–78.

Hope, Murry. *The Way of Cartouche: An Oracle of Ancient Egyptian Magic.* New York: St. Martin's Press, 1985.

Joe Versus the Volcano. Written by John Patrick Shanley, Directed by John Patrick Shanley. Burbank, CA: Warner Brothers Entertainment, Amblin Entertainment, 1990.

Judith, Anodea. *Wheels of Life: A User's Guide to the Chakra System.* Woodbury, MN: Llewellyn Publications, 1987.

Jung, Carl. *Synchronicity: An Acausal Connecting Principle.* New York: Routledge, 2008.

Jung, Sharon Jiyoon, Hyunji Gil, Dong-Hyun Kim, Hong-Lim Kim, Sungchul Kim, and Kwang-Sup Soh. 2016. "Ultrastructure of a Mobile Threadlike Tissue Floating in a Lymph Vessel." *Evidence-Based Complementary and Alternative Medicine.* 2016:1–5.

Kabat-Zinn, Jon. *Mindfulness for Beginners: Reclaiming the Present Moment—And Your Life.* Boulder, CO: Sounds True, 2002.

Keel, John A. *The Mothman Prophecies.* New York: Tor Books, 1975.

Marciniak, Barbara. *Bringers of the Dawn: Teachings from the Pleiadians.* Rochester, VT: Bear & Company, 1992.

Martin, Francois, Federico Carminati, and Giuliana Galli Carminati. 2009. "Synchronicity, Quantum Information and the Psyche." *Journal of Cosmology* 3:580– 589.

Myss, Caroline. *Sacred Contracts: Awakening Your Divine Potential.* New York: Harmony Books, 2003.

Ram Dass. *Ram Dass Audio Collection: A Collection of Three Ram Dass Favorites-- Conscious Aging, The Path of Service, and Cultivating the Heart of Compassion.* Boulder, CO: Sounds True, 2000.

Ramirez-Oropeza, Martha and William Douglas Horden. *The Toltec I Ching.* Burdett, NY: Larson Publications, 2009.

Richardson, Cheryl. *Grace Cards.* New York: Hay House, 2005.

Ruiz, Don Miguel. *The Four Agreements A Practical Guide to Personal Freedom (A Toltec Wisdom Book).* San Rafael, CA: Amber-Allen Publishing, 1997.

Smith, Paul H. *Coordinate Remote Viewing Training Manual.* Washington, DC: Defense Intelligence Agency Press, 1986.

Swann, Ingo. *On-Going Scientific Discovery of Sensory Receptors Which Account for Many Subtle Perceptions.* September 12, 1996. Paper presented to the United Nations, on March, 21, 1994. HYPERLINK "http://www.ingoswann.com/un-paper.html" http://www.ingoswann.com/un-paper.html

_____. *Reality Boxes and Other Black Holes in Human Consciousness.* New York: Ingo Swann Books, 2003.

Targ, Russell. *Limitless Mind: A Guide to Remote viewing and Transformation of Consciousness.* Novato, CA: New World Library, 2004.

Targ, Russell. *The Reality of ESP: A Physicist's Proof of Psychic Abilities.* Wheaton, IL: Quest Books, 2012.

Waldinger, Robert. *What Makes a Good Life? Lessons on the Longest Study on Happiness.* TEDxBeaconStreet, 2015. https://www.ted.com/talks/robert_waldinger_what_makes_a_good_life_lessons_from_th e_longest_study_on_happiness

Wilhelm, Richard. *The I Ching, Or, Book Of Changes—The Richard Wilhelm Translation*. Princeton, NJ: Princeton University Press, 1997.

Williams, Dana. *The Lord's Prayer, The Seven Chakras, The Twelve Life Paths: The Prayer of Christ Consciousness as a Light for the Auric Centers and a Map through the Archetypal Life Paths of Astrology*. USA: Attunement Press, 2009.

Wilson, Colin. *Mysteries: An Investigation into the Occult, the Paranormal and the Supernatural*. London: Watkins Publishing, 2006.

www.ingramcontent.com/pod-product-compliance
Lightning Source LLC
Chambersburg PA
CBHW021146080526
44588CB00008B/239